The Best of Times

The Best of Times

by Philbrook Paine

YANKEE, *Inc.*

Dublin, New Hampshire

Book design: John White
Illustrations: Gordon Heckman

Yankee, Inc., Dublin, New Hampshire 03444
First Edition
Copyright 1981, by Yankee, Inc.
Printed in the United States of America

Library of Congress Catalog Card No. 81-52195
ISBN 0-911658-32-7

To Serena

Contents

The author (on the right), his twin brother Stuart, and their mother, about 1922.

Introduction

AT the age of sixty-six, a man can recall certain things that happened half a century before. If his memory goes back much further than that, you may be pretty sure that he is embellishing events he has merely heard about, or else he is fabricating from an active imagination. In the latter case he is a fiction artist and should label his stuff so. On the other hand, if a man my age says that he can recall the time when the family car was jacked up on blocks of wood for the winter months, he is probably making a simple statement of fact. Thus, he becomes a purveyor of slightly colored nostalgia.

I like to think that I fall into that category. I was born in the age of kerosene lamps, real horse power, the one-cylinder engine, and the coal furnace. At ten, I was unaware that every kid would someday carry a transistor radio with him on the way to school. I failed to foresee the miniskirt, or television, or the computer, or space travel. But I knew a lot about woodchucks. And they haven't changed much during the past half century.

The interval I remember most kindly was the first part of the 1920s. A lot has been said about these days. The shortening skirts, the hip flasks, the raccoon coats, and the Lost

Generation. Love had been removed from the porch swing and taken out to the Model T touring car. Everything was going to pot behind four-cylinder gasoline engines.

I recall small evidence of this upheaval because so little of it reached out to the farm. Once I did hear my father telling my mother about the new era after he had returned from a trip to New York. "One sniff of a rotten apple," he said, "and they're lurching all over the railroad cars and making fools of themselves. A bunch of them got off at New Haven, and they made me ashamed of the new Yale. Now in my day . . . ." In his day, it seemed, things had been different. His generation consumed small quantities of ale at a place called Mory's, and then they sang good, solid Yale songs. I wasn't much concerned with the problem, but I think he was intimating to my mother that the college generation then was having trouble holding its likker.

From the ages of ten to fifteen, however, I didn't have much time to ponder whether the post-war generation was getting lost or just beginning to find itself. So many new things were coming along so fast. Electric power, fox traps, girls, and earphones. At the same time we were still clinging to the latter part of the nineteenth century.

We retained the cows and the hens and the pigs. We cut our own ice in the winter, and we hayed our fields. For the benefit of the cows, we still kept a bull, though at the time I was skeptical of Lawrence Page's account of how it earned its living.

And I do remember that, for several years, the car was jacked up on wooden blocks in November and put back on the ground in April. During the winter months, we rode into town in either a sleigh or a buggy behind Charley Horse or the black pony. The rest of the time, my twin brother Stuart and I walked or bicycled the mile to school. I am aware that everybody over the age of fifty trudged to school in his youth with varying degrees of hardiness. The written record, so far as I know from my own reading, is nine miles each way. But at our school, nobody had to walk more than five miles to study his sums. And except when there was snow on the ground, the usual form of transportation was the bicycle. I believe that I could this minute take a New Departure brake apart blindfolded.

I wish I could state truthfully that we were poor but simple country folk, gaining a meager living from a New Hampshire hardscrabble farm. We weren't. My father earned a splendid income at his typewriter. A Canadian girl named Violet held sway in the kitchen, and there was usually a hired man hiding around the place somewhere. But somehow we had to do all the things that current literature says simple country folk did then.

We separated the cream from the milk by means of a hand-propelled separator. My daughter doesn't know what a separator is. Some time ago, when I explained about the disks and centrifugal force, she thought I was getting into the theory of relativity. I tried to instruct as well as entertain her with a detailed account of churning butter in the old kitchen. I imitated the *slap-slap* of the paddles going around in the churn, as well as the feel of the handle as the butter began to form into lumps. In pantomime, I drained off the buttermilk and lifted out the chunk of butter so that she would know what it was like when I was young. I told her how we pressed the fatty substance and added the salt and coloring. "Huh," she said. I guess she just wasn't interested in butter.

Nowadays, I get to see quite a bit of young people who are two generations from the 1920s. They are more studious than we were. The energy they devote to extracurricular affairs is astonishing. They can boogaloo and play clarinets and tennis, and they swim and they can act. But when they correspond on paper, they have trouble getting a singular or plural subject to jibe with the verb.

My mother was always talking about the development of our inner resources. Several decades passed before I understood what she meant. The sentence I hear most often from the current crop of youngsters is, "What shall we do now?" My mother would have replied, "Find a book and read it."

The boys who grew up on farms in an earlier era never had to ask, "What shall we do now?" We were hard pressed to find time to complete our projects. Despite the various hired men who lurked around the barn from time to time, my brother and I milked the cows, chased the cows when they got over the fence, mowed lawns, tilled gardens, and dismantled perfectly good alarm clocks. We also were required to read. At

11

six, I probably knew as much about Old Mother West Wind as Mr. Burgess himself. Nowadays, a youngster of similar age is more likely watching "The Beverly Hillbillies," without the least comprehension of what went on in the Green Meadows forty years ago.

It is hard for more recent generations to conceive of life as it was for their parents and grandparents fifty years ago. No electricity, no television, only faint howls from the radio, few automobiles, no thermostats, no electric blankets, no school buses, and no stereos. But of course we weren't aware of what we were missing. When Caruso's voice came scratching out of the phonograph's big horn on which was depicted a dog with the slogan "His Master's Voice," we thought civilization had gone about as far as it ought to go, or ever would.

Obviously the new generation is bright. I see evidence of it every day. They handle words like "trauma" and "ecology" without batting an eye. But they don't know how to put a bit into a horse's mouth on a frosty morning, or chase a pig, or salt down green beans in an earthen crock. And they live in ignorance of one of the great triumphs of early-twentieth-century science, the Smith Motor Wheel. This is the sort of knowledge that only a few of us still possess.

There was nothing especially unusual about the town in which I grew up, except that it was the home of the New Hampshire College of Agriculture and the Mechanic Arts, as the University of New Hampshire was then known. In those days there was no separation of town and gown. If Ed Chesley, the road agent, received more complaints than he thought necessary from the residents of Faculty Road, the professors might find their driveways barricaded with snow while the rest of Durham moved freely on bare roads, but there was no anti-college sentiment in this. Ed would be the first to recruit undergraduate votes to kill an article in the town warrant that threatened higher taxes. Altogether, there was a lot of nice give and take between the two groups before microphones and loud-speakers were installed in front of the moderator's desk.

Nor was there anything unusual about our farm, except that it was named Shankhassick. This is supposed to mean "wild goose" in an Indian tongue and to be an Indian name for the saltwater river that runs up to Durham. The white settlers renamed it the Oyster River, thus allowing my father to borrow the earlier name for the farm he purchased here in 1907.

The thing I remember best about my boyhood on the farm is the wide-eyed attention we gave to each new miracle as it came down the driveway. Whether it was a utility line carrying the new power, or a double-acting Lunt Moss pump, our reaction was, "Gee whiz, what's next?" In the short interval between 1920 and 1925, our mode of living changed from agrarian nineteenth century to very nearly what it is now. Of course, there were winter days when we shut off certain rooms in the old house because we couldn't heat them with a coal furnace ... but we did the same thing yesterday despite two oil-fired brutes.

Readers who were born more recently may find some sticky words in the following pages, though in most cases I have tried to explain them along the way. For example, take running boards. They haven't been used on automobiles for forty years, unless you count the Volkswagen beetle as an automobile. Similarly, the one-lunger gave out its final pop around 1937. The pung passed from view in the late twenties. To an older generation all these were as common as electronic calculators are to today's young people.

However, if doubt does arise about the meaning of an old-fashioned term, my advice is to ask somebody who was born on a New England farm around 1910. He'll know.

chapter one

The Sons
of Daniel Boone

ALMOST every kid in America, except me, grew up hanging around a drugstore. My absence wasn't because Durham didn't have a drugstore — it did. Jim Gorman owned it. And I guess it was a pretty good drugstore to hang around, from all reports. Perhaps not the biggest drugstore in the world, but certainly not the smallest, either. Kind of a fair-to-middling type of drugstore.

There were lots of good reasons why I didn't want to hang around Jim Gorman's emporium. For example, he only sold milk shakes, Moxie, and birch beer. They were good enough for kids, perhaps, but nothing that a true Son of Daniel Boone would go wild about.

For the fact was that our local chapter of the Sons of Daniel Boone was devoted to the manufacture and consumption of native wine. The enterprise was brought about, in an indirect way, by the Boy Scouts of America. There were four of us Tenderfeet who bought our scout uniforms, carried jackknives, and tried to do at least one turn a day, good or bad, for some old lady. But at the end of six months, about all we had learned was how to extinguish a campfire without going down to the brook for water. So we quit in a group and embraced the banner of Daniel Boone.

We met in a hayloft after school on Tuesday afternoons and elected our officers. Then we whittled a little, and fought with each other, and returned home, inspired and uplifted by the spirit of the great Indian scout.

Just when the club was being threatened by extinction for the lack of a program, we accidentally stumbled on a splendid vineyard of wild grapes. They grew on a cliff behind Lawrence Page's house. They were smaller than the cultivated grapes we occasionally saw on the table at home, and they were a little tart. But indisputably they were grapes. Every one of us was aware that the French tilled their vineyards and made wine and inevitably came to bad ends.

Prohibition was then getting underway, so everybody was pretty interested in what happened when alcohol was introduced into the human stomach. The Eighteenth Amendment was a sure-fire attention-grabber in that respect; it all but forced us to experiment a little on our own with the pitfalls of alcohol.

The Sons of Daniel Boone were a crafty bunch. We knew the value of stealth, silence, and deviousness. So we didn't just lug a great basket of grapes up the driveway and into the hayloft. My mother surely would have inquired why four boys thought they could eat twelve thousand grapes on a Tuesday afternoon. She was one of the few who believed in the Volstead Act,* and she might have suspected what we had in mind.

No, we Sons of Daniel Boone stripped the vineyard and brought our grapes back to the barn in small quantities along secret trails, being careful not to leave any broken twigs behind us. Then we set up our winery in the hayloft. The principal machinery required was a twenty-quart stone jar, formerly used for salting down green beans; a rounded wooden instrument that under normal conditions was employed in the manufacture of cottage cheese; and a large colander that fitted over the top of the crock.

So while the Boy Scouts were busy in the village helping old ladies across streets, the Sons of Daniel Boone squatted

---

*The Volstead Act was the 1919 act of Congress providing for Federal enforcement of Prohibition.

there in the semidarkness of the hayloft and crushed grapes into the crock. Actually, it was a fairly arduous task. By the end of the afternoon, we figured maybe the French came to their bad ends not so much from drinking wine as from trying to squeeze the juice out of grapes.

That meeting lasted a long time. When we eventually disbanded around six o'clock, the crock was three-quarters full of clear, unsweetened grape juice. We put the top on and left it to do whatever it was supposed to do. If our information was correct, by the time the next meeting rolled around the following Tuesday, this pale, tart, innocent-looking fluid would be ready to turn us into drunkards before we could say Daniel Boone.

Well, the seven days passed with an intolerable slowness, but then it was Tuesday afternoon again, and our boys' club climbed stealthily up to the hayloft to sample our "program."

To get at it, we had to remove quite a bit of foul-looking mold, but Normy Glidden guessed that the mold was probably a good thing. This opinion elevated him somewhat in our eyes, so we let him take the first swig. Our faith in our product was such that we expected him to turn into a drunkard right then and there, after which it would be our turn.

As we watched hopefully, Normy drained his glass and fell down. Then he clutched his throat and wiped his eyes, and exclaimed, "Wow!"

"Boy!" we said. "He's drunk. One glass and he's a drunkard. Gimme the glass."

One by one we broke the Volstead Act until we were all sitting on the floor beside Normy, wiping our eyes and rubbing our throats. "Some stuff!" we agreed.

None of us would admit that our wine tasted like vinegar, and that our throat holding and eye wiping were due entirely to its dismaying tartness. As for its ability to lead us down the long and hopeless road to a drunkard's end, it was a fizzle. We might just as well have each tossed down a glass of fresh lemon juice. But we had nobody to tell us that. We just thought we were hardened drinkers, breaking the law and heading for bad ends.

The Sons of Daniel Boone continued with this "program" well into the fall. At successive meetings we would add sugar and yeast, and skim the mold from the top. Then we would go through our ritual of downing a glass of the bitter stuff before electing new officers. Once in a while, the ritual would be modified a little by a heated investigation into the question of "who left the goddamn top off?"

This seemed important at the time, and, as things turned out, it was. By the time the weather began to get too cold in the hayloft for any lengthy gatherings of the Boone boys, the "program" was almost finished anyway. The contents of the crock had been lowered to within a couple of inches of the bottom, and it was about time to disband.

At our final meeting, we pegged away at the vinegar for a while, then decided to destroy the evidence. Daniel Boone wouldn't have left anything around for the Indians to find. No, sir. So we lowered the crock out a window to the ground and tipped it over. It was a pretty seedy-looking winery by now. A little of the remaining juice ran out; then some undissolved sugar, a little hay, and finally three dead mice in a state of considerable disrepair.

Quite a few years passed before I drank any wine again, but it was uplifting projects like the Sons of Daniel Boone that kept me from hanging around drugstores and getting corrupted.

chapter two

Getting Religion

SOON after the wine debacle a bunch of Durham youths got religion.

The Sunday-school superintendent at the community church gave out the word. And the message he brought was a simple one. The Sunday-school class that contributed the most money to the weekly collection throughout the winter would be rewarded with a trip to Boston and a big-league baseball game in the spring. All expenses would be on the church, so to speak, including the popcorn. To make the reward seem even more colossal, the game would be played between the Red Sox and the Yankees.

This last was about as close to heaven as any of our hardy band could visualize. Although we were equally divided concerning our loyalties to the Red Sox and the Yankees, all of us could see the merit of joining forces until May.

On the Sunday when this stupendous announcement was made, only four young disciples were on hand to receive the news. But it didn't take long for the word to spread. It traveled down to Durham Point and along the Newmarket Road, inspiring a religious fervor equaled only when, a few years later,

Mon Whitney saw God in a coal furnace at the reform school and jumped in after him.

It was on this particular fall afternoon that Mon had his first vision, and it led straight to the Red Sox ballpark. The news likewise electrified the Paine twins, the three Chamberlin boys, Squeak Perley, and Chickie Hatch, as well as Lawrence Page and young Tater Watson. On the other side of the river, Herbie Jackson (who kept snakes in his pockets) turned to God before the afternoon was over; and in the village Robbie Robinson felt the call.

The following Sunday, twelve youngsters who had declared themselves for a better and fuller religious life showed up in a group. The superintendent appeared gratified, and our teacher, a Miss May who had never seen so many boys gathered together under that holy roof, fairly cackled in her delight.

Nowadays, I think we would be called "motivated." At that time, however, we were merely crooked. A good share of the considerable sum that went into the collection that first Sunday was "hot" money. The dollar bill I put in for the greater glory of the Red Sox had been found on my father's bureau. The others resorted to similar stratagems: loose change in a parental pocket, a quarter behind a chair cushion, a little something out of Mother's purse. But it added up. One or two had learned commerce right along with the gospel. By selling their fathers' cigarettes at a cut-rate price to the older boys, they were able to contribute their share to the church. Only Mon Whitney, who was an old fashioned poverty pocket all by himself, had to resort to stealing outside the family. But he was accomplished at his trade, and sometimes contributed more than we better-heeled religious fanatics.

All in all that first Sunday's take was a little over twelve dollars, an astonishing amount for a group that the previous week had only managed to put aside seventeen cents for His use.

Our fervor burned like a clear white light throughout the winter. Nothing could stop us. No matter how deep the drifts, we put on our snowshoes and struggled through blizzards to hear Miss May's personal interpretation of the Book. To be candid, this was not exactly an inspiring exercise, and she could have spent her Sunday mornings more profitably by reading the sports pages to us. Because that is what some of us did anyway. As our little thieveries kept our collection-box score in top place, we began to follow the fortunes of the baseball world more avidly. Any news of the Red Sox or Yankees made the story of the Resurrection look pretty pale by comparison.

But then, one Sunday in April, we received a rude shock. It was reported that a class of slightly older would-be saints was nudging us from first place in the Sunday-school collection standings. Could we meet the challenge? Were we to be vanquished after six long and arduous months of crime? It hardly seemed fair. Some of us began to have serious doubts about how God worked in His wondrous ways.

As the final Sunday drew near before the pennant race would be decided, our little band redoubled its efforts. We stole more heavily from our parents; we sold our jackknives; and we played fast and loose with the grocery money. We even borrowed legally. That proved how much we anticipated the trip to Boston.

The last collection should have caused some eyebrow raising in the Sunday-school hierarchy. Maybe it did; I don't know. Or perhaps the hierarchy was as crooked as we, because in those days twelve boys, no matter how strong their religious zeal, just didn't drop twenty-five dollars into a Sunday-school collection box.

But it was enough to clinch the pennant. We went to Boston in three cars, driven by good devout people, including my father, and we saw the ball game. I have forgotten the score, but it was immaterial. The main thing was, we had seen a big-league baseball game.

It was the last big-league baseball game I ever attended. The previous Sunday also went into the record books: it was the last Sunday-school class that our little band attended.

To compensate for the loss, however, most of us gave up stealing.

chapter three

Joy to the World

ONE December, word came down from the parents of certain youths in the village that there was a lot more to Christmas than opening presents with frantic haste. The Yuletide spirit was the thing. This meant giving to the less-fortunate members of the community. Furthermore, it meant giving something of ourselves — something we couldn't simply buy at a store and have wrapped. We were to spread joy amongst the shut-ins on Christmas Eve.

Probably no more diabolical form of spreading joy was ever inflicted on five or six families who didn't deserve such a fate. About ten of us were formed into a caroling group. We were to learn the words to "Silent Night" and "We Three Kings" and hike around the town to the homes where the less fortunate lived. Then we were to go into the houses to cheer the hearts of the lonely old people by singing about frankincense and myrrh.

We learned the words after a fashion, but, although we had been singing the carols at school since the middle of December, we were having trouble with the tunes. For it was a fact that no ten boys in history had ever been born so tone deaf; we were able to move into "Silent Night" from the middle of "We Three Kings" without being aware of it. Nevertheless, we were young, our faces were bright, and we had enthusiasm. This last hinged principally on an obsession to get inside Lizzie Brown's house.

Getting inside the house was the only way we knew to see Lizzie Brown with her coat off. For she never appeared outside her home without a coat, winter or summer. Because of this, it was rumored in the school yard with some authority that she wore her coat to cover up a medical wonder so fascinating, so unique, and so incredible that our young minds were hard put to take it in.

She was alleged to carry her intestines about in a bag.

To our delight, Lizzie and her husband were prime targets for our Christmas Eve caroling group. They were old and they were bent and they needed cheering up. All of us heard our parents discussing the circumstances in which this aging and near-destitute couple found themselves.

There were several other families who needed a touch of Christmas joy, but the Browns were the *pièce de résistance* of the evening. By some sort of common instinct, we decided to cheer them last.

So off we went through the snow and cold to improve the spiritual tone of the town's least-likely-to-succeed. We first stopped at an elderly spinster's home and rendered "Silent Night" while she looked askance at our snowy boots that were making puddles on her hand-scrubbed floor. From there we pushed on to a home where the husband was reportedly ill and in bed. He wasn't in bed, but there was little doubt that he was ill. He greeted us warmly and invited us in, and even offered us some of the medicine he was taking from a large bottle. We were glad we had come to cheer him up this Christmas Eve because he was so sick he stumbled over a chair a couple of times and then fell down in a corner of the living room. Observing such a terrible sickness made us give out with everything we had. And that gallant man, despite his pain, joined us from his corner, and took another swig of medicine.

Exhilarated by this experience in spreading joy among the sick and shut-in, we trooped on through the night to still another unfortunate. This was a widow woman who scrubbed floors at the college. She fed us cookies and apples and said not to worry about the snow that was melting. After we finished our caroling, Squeak Perley jostled Chickie Hatch, and the widow woman was minus one chair. We bolted for the door, all trying to get through it at one time, and headed for the Browns'.

On the way, there was considerable speculation among us as to what we were going to find. Was the bag tied around her shoulders? Or did it hang from the waist? Guesses were made about the number of feet of intestine that lay in the bag. Five, ten, twenty? This held our attention until we had passed over the bridge and were in sight of the house. Then a numbing awe fell over us as we contemplated what we were about to see. If it turned out to be true, our labors would not have been in vain. Furthermore, it would be a news scoop that would make the other kids wish they had gone into the caroling business.

From the outside, the house was squalid, even though none of us at the time knew what the word meant. But there was a lamp burning in one room, which indicated that the Browns were still up. We rapped timidly on the door and waited with our mouths dry. There was a muffled murmuring inside, and then we heard somebody coming to open it. Mr. Brown pulled it back and thrust a lamp into our faces.

"Mr. Brown," I said fearfully, "we've come to sing you some Christmas carols."

"Delighted," boomed Mr. Brown, his great white beard moving up and down. "Come in, gentlemen, and a Merry Christmas to you."

We marched in, pushing and shoving the way twelve year olds do, and stood about silently for a moment. Whereupon Mr. Brown said, "Wait, boys, before you sing. I'll call Mrs. Brown down. This is something she must see." He went to a doorway that led upstairs and called to her. She answered, and we could hear the blood pounding in our ears. Within a moment or two, we would know for sure. And during this moment, we had a chance to observe that even if the outside of the house was run-down, the inside was immaculate.

Mr. Brown stood beside the stairway door, waiting for his

wife to appear, and we remained motionless, staring at it with our eyes fairly popping out of their sockets. We heard her first footsteps on the top stairs, and then she started to descend. Mr. Brown leaned up to help her, saying, "Boys, this is Mrs. Brown. Lizzie, they've come to sing to us, bless their hearts."

There she was, beaming at us from the doorway. An audible gasp escaped from ten throats. *She was wearing a coat.* This, despite the fact that the room was overheated from a wood stove that was crackling in the corner. I don't know if our disappointment showed too plainly, or whether we just appeared to be shy and embarrassed. In any event, she said immediately, "Well, boys, let's hear you sing. I'll join you. What will it be? 'Silent Night'?"

We nodded dumbly. She came over close to us and raised her arms. "All right now," she said, "all together!" and we started in creating our usual carnage with "Silent Night." But there was something about her voice that carried us along on key for the whole stretch. When it was finished, she said, "Wonderful, boys. Now what else do you know?" Chickie Hatch told a fib and said we knew "We Three Kings." Again, she led us through one of our finest moments. Seven or eight of us stayed on key right through to the end.

After that, she brought out doughnuts and cider from the kitchen, and we wolfed them down as though we were the destitute ones on Christmas Eve. But our hunger did not prevent ten pairs of eyes studying Lizzie's profile from head to toe. Then the Browns wished us a Merry Christmas and thanked us for walking out to sing our carols.

On the way home, we had to admit — as quietly as twelve-year-old boys can on a frosty night — that Lizzie's insides were right where they were supposed to be. As for the coat, well, we now understood that she kept it on, winter and summer, inside the house and out, to cover the one faded, patched, but scrubbed dress she planned to be buried in.

Our mothers could have told us that before we formed the caroling group.

chapter four

The Smith Motor Wheel

 M Y older brother sent away for a Savage twenty-two
rifle. It was a thing of beauty and about the size of those used
in World War I. Ostensibly, this magnificent new firearm was
to be employed in target shooting. So Del tacked a bullseye up
on a hickory tree that stood alone in the middle of the field,
and he and Sam Hoitt and Jim Smart banged away at it for
almost an hour.

By that time target shooting had lost its novelty, and they
began to look around for something livelier to shoot at. As it
happened, a gray squirrel had been gathering nuts near the top
of the tree, and he started to scold the intruders below. He
would have done better to have kept his complaints to himself. The boys used half a box of bullets to bring him down,
but eventually they did, and they stretched his pelt on a
shingle in the woodshed. From that moment on, they
declared war on squirrels. In an indirect way, their new enterprise started me toward the eventual culmination of my fond-
est dream: the possession of a Smith Motor Wheel that Mon
Whitney had acquired in some mysterious way, probably illegal.

The Smith Motor Wheel was an ingenious piece of

machinery, the grandfather of millions of Yahamas and Hondas that now make popping noises along the world's streets and byways. It was a self-contained affair. The one cylinder was mounted on a single rubber-tired wheel, which could be attached to the frame of any standard bicycle. The throttle wire ran to the one handlebar. By squeezing it properly, the operator was alleged to be able to obtain speeds as high as thirty miles per hour. All the boys' magazines were liberally sprinkled with advertisements for this marvelous machine that would eliminate pumping uphill.

The copywriters who turned out those ads understood human psychology, particularly the wants and needs of a boy. I kept one of their ads beside my bed at all times. It showed a youngster merrily whizzing up a hill. This lucky fellow was waving to a group of his friends who had dismounted from their bikes and were pushing them laboriously up the grade. My sole ambition for a time was to be that boy on the Smith Motor Wheel.

Mon Whitney had one in his barn. About once a week, I went home with him after school to gaze upon it with envy and adoration. It was the most magnificent piece of machinery I had ever seen. Mon said his brother had given it to him before disappearing on one of his frequent journeys to places unknown. Mon's brother often found the climate more congenial elsewhere than it was in his home town.

However, the origin of this red miracle in the barn did not trouble me, and Mon was willing to part with it for ten dollars. I even believed his story, that he didn't attach it to his own bike because "the frame ain't strong enough." When I suggested that we hang it on my bike in order to try it out, he explained that the tire was flat or "there ain't no gas in the tank." He always had some excuse why I couldn't get my hands on that Smith Motor Wheel without paying him ten dollars.

The day my brother shot his first squirrel in the hickory tree proved to be the turning point for me and modern transportation. He and his friends went on to become the most expert squirrel hunters on Durham Point. For a while thereafter, anything gray that moved in a tree did not live long enough to have any regrets. The group cleaned out all the squirrels on our land, except possibly for one or two that worked at night. Then my brother and his fellow hunters worked over Mr. Page's field and stone wall until the woodshed was festooned with skins. Furs look pretty on women and no doubt add a good deal to fashion, but draped inside out on a woodshed wall they are less attractive. Furthermore, a fur coat in its earlier stages of development gives off a peculiar odor. It can't compete with a damp buffalo robe, but it can certainly lay claim to second place.

As a result of this carnage, when fall came and the weather grew colder, a vast supply of hickory nuts lay under the trees, unclaimed. At that time we had thirty or more hickories within a hundred-yard radius of the barn. They produced nuts in such quantities that it appeared the trees thought they were the last ones on earth. Or maybe nature figured on the squirrels and got the hickories to produce enough for them, with a few left over for propagating the species. Whatever their motive, the big old trees showered down a bumper crop that fall. With all competition from the squirrels eliminated, I had no trouble in filling a ten-quart pail in an hour.

Now, the home consumption of nuts never exceeded more than six or seven per winter. I am referring to nuts, not quarts. If you are young and curious, are equipped with a hammer and a pick, and haven't anything better to do for an hour or two, it is possible to extract some nourishment from a hickory nut. Or if you were starving under a hickory tree, and you worked steadily for eighteen hours a day, you might be able to fend off the end for two days or so.

Motivated, however, by the Smith Motor Wheel, I sold forty quarts of those nuts to my family's friends. It was pure swindle. Mrs. Belle Mathes bought four quarts; she probably threw them out the back door before I reached the next prospect. Bill Chamberlin's father took a similar number of quarts because my father had subscribed to three magazines when Bill was starting his own career in commerce.*

And so it went, up and down Main Street, from the town hall to the railroad station. Charlie Wentworth bought a cou-

---

*A few years ago, I bought a package of rare seeds from Mr. Chamberlin's grandson. They didn't come up, but he got his Spaceman's Watch.

ple of quarts to help while away the time between trains. Frank Morrison, who ran the livery stable, was good for six quarts because he had a soft spot for growing kids. Runlett's store paid the retail price for three quarts and tried to give them away to customers, but couldn't.

It all added up to ten dollars. With the cash in my pocket, I set off to negotiate with Mon Whitney. He was a little secretive about the exchange, peering through the barn door occasionally to check the appearance of his house. This may have had something to do with the true ownership of the Smith Motor Wheel, or perhaps Mon was afraid my ten dollars would pass through his hands and into his mother's before he could put it to use. But after we bolted the machine on and rigged the throttle that was going to assure me speeds up to thirty miles per hour, Mon gave his house a final inspection and announced that the coast was clear. In another moment, I was going to be the kid on the Smith Motor Wheel, waving merrily to less-fortunate contemporaries.

Alas, Mon had been right about a couple of things. The tire was soft and the gas tank was empty. So instead of pushing just the bike up the long grade to Fred Knight's garage, I also had to lug the Smith Motor Wheel.

Fred Knight thought the machine was quite a gadget. He filled the tank and inflated the tire. Then he tinkered with the choke and wrapped a few things with baling wire, and guessed it was ready to go.

It wasn't. I pumped the pedals all the way down the first hill without so much as a pop. The machine made noises all right, but not the kind that indicate exploding gasoline. It just chuffed. The discouraging sort of *chuff, chuff, chuff* of a piston going up and down without any intention of helping to supply the power.

When I finally pushed it up the driveway, more tired than I would have been if I had ridden the bike twenty miles, I was beginning to feel discouraged. Dick O'Kane came down the next day and offered a suggestion. Why not detach it from the bicycle and spike it to an upright timber in the barn? Then we wouldn't have to work on it through the spokes of a wheel. This also left the bike free for me to ride in the meantime without helping the Smith Motor Wheel along.

34

For a week after that we spun the Wheel, unscrewed things, tightened bolts, and spilled gasoline around the barn. The spark plug, which was removed every eight minutes to prime the cyclinder, became round from the gnawing of a Jesus wrench. Still no action.

Then Dick made his second suggestion. Why not try some ether? His father was an entomologist whose laboratory contained a can of this highly combustible fluid. Next day, the laboratory didn't contain any ether. It was being poured into my Smith Motor Wheel. The barn smelled like an operating room.

"All right," Dick said, "pull the wheel over. By gosh, I'll bet she'll go this time." He was a prophet.

We were so conditioned to failure that we couldn't believe our eyes. The exhaust pipe gave off a blast of ether fumes, and the Wheel started turning at a very high rate of speed — so high, indeed, that the vibration caused the spikes to pull out of the post. This yanked the throttle cable from its nails and opened it wide. When the machine finally met the floor, it bounced five feet into the air and came down again with its ears laid back. It looked like a cat trying to find traction on a piece of glass. As soon as the Smith Motor Wheel discovered that it was basically intended to operate on land, it shot through the barn door, hit a rock, and crashed over on its side.

Here it went through its final moments, gyrating around on the ground like an eel. Dick and I were so impressed by our handiwork that neither of us had moved, but now we ran over and tried to shut it off. We were too late. The same amazing qualities of ether that had breathed life into the worn-out engine were now being investigated by the exhaust pipe. The top of the fuel tank had come off at the first bounce, and the ether was trickling down to areas where it had no business to be.

At the first sight of flame, Dick and I departed. We covered twenty feet before the explosion came. The fuel tank went first, followed by minor eruptions in the carburetor and fuel line. These in turn ignited the tire. After that, we just squatted down and watched it burn. There were lots of things on that Smith Motor Wheel that were combustible. Almost an hour passed before we could get near enough to examine the wreckage, and there wasn't much left. Just some hot metal.

Dick's parting observation was, "I *thought* ether would do the trick."

Although I never had the fun of waving merrily to the other boys as I sped by on my Smith Motor Wheel, I did have the satisfaction of owning one for a week. That was more than my friends could say, unless I included Mon Whitney. Moreover, I was able to understand one thing more clearly. If Mon's brother really had given him the machine, I now knew why.

chapter five

Stunting Our Growth

HALF a century before the Surgeon General discovered that smoke from burning tobacco leaves can injure the delicate and marvelously complex tissues of the human lung, lots of people were warning us that "smoking will stunt your growth."

Shorty Gould was the living proof. He was in our grade at school, and he smoked anything that could be lighted, particularly somebody else's butts. He was a foot shorter than most of us. Thus the cause and the effect were plainly visible to anybody who believed in the stunt-your-growth theory. Most parents believed in it and passed the information along to growing boys.

Unfortunately for the theory, when Shorty Gould turned thirteen, he began to shoot up. His voice changed to a deep growl, and his pants began to grow away from his shoes.

During this interval when Shorty was exploding the stunt-your-growth theory, he smoked with increasing enthusiasm. Moreover, his collection system became better organized. Through trial and error, he sought out the places where the longest butts were likely to be found. The railroad station was one of these. Passengers as a rule lighted their cigarettes when the locomotive whistled for the Madbury crossing, giving them time for a few final drags before getting onto the train. Then they flipped their butts onto the track and went their ways. An alert kid like Shorty could pick up a day's supply after the seven-thirty-three pulled out toward Boston.

Another good place was the Community Church, although this was only worthwhile on Sundays. For some reason, men who were about to receive spiritual salvation felt a craving for nicotine right up to the door of the church. There was a narrow sidewalk leading to the door, bordered by grass on the left side. Few members of the congregation wanted to be caught dropping cigarettes on the very steps of the church, so they surreptitiously tossed them onto the grass. The better people of the town attended Sunday devotions, and as a rule the brands were good. Shorty then made his own collection outside the church, accompanied by the thundering notes of "Onward, Christian Soldiers!"

By the time he had stunted his growth at six feet four inches, it was pretty plain to all of us that tobacco and height had little or no relationship. The health-minded members of the community were finding it difficult to hold Shorty Gould up as the horrible example, especially since he towered above everybody at school and all but two or three men in the community.

After the stunt-your-growth campaign fizzled out, we were warned that smoking would "cut your wind." Just why cutting our wind was injurious wasn't made entirely clear. We had no organized cross-country team — a dubious sort of endeavor anyway — where lung power might have been a factor, and our baseball activities were mostly conducted in the long grass behind Fred Knight's garage, looking for the ball.

So it was a losing battle from the start. Our parents didn't have the Surgeon General to back them up by obliging cigarette manufacturers to print his health warning on every package. This, I imagine, deters millions of Shorty Goulds from embracing the evil habit. Except of course that Shorty would never have seen a whole pack of cigarettes at one time.

In any event, so much had been said about tobacco by the time I was fifteen that I suspected it had certain virtues. Otherwise I don't believe I would have given it a second thought.

Bill Chamberlin was of a similar mind, so we planned a camping trip to an island in Great Bay where we could be at liberty to try the weed for ourselves.

We packed a tent and a few blankets and some canned goods in the bottom of the sailboat. These were the non-essentials. The most precious part of our cargo was stowed in a metal strongbox that my family normally used for keys that didn't fit any locks, and for other equally valuable assets.

In this were six different makes of cigarettes, plus a bundle of kitchen matches. All of the then popular brands were included, as well as a pack of Turkish Delights that Bill's father enjoyed. Our object was a complete survey of the tobacco industry, which we intended to accomplish in three days.

After sailing to the island, we pitched our tent and set up our sketchy housekeeping arrangements. When these chores were completed, we opened the strongbox and went to work. We began with the Lucky Strikes. ("Reach for a Lucky instead of a sweet!") We got them lighted and drew the smoke into our mouths. We immediately blew it out and spat through the tent opening.

"Great stuff," Bill said, spitting again.

We took another drag, whereupon I got a little smoke into my throat. This set up a coughing spell that lasted ten minutes, by which time our cigarettes had burned down to their ends.

"Here, Bill," I said, holding out the Lucky Strikes, "have another. We've got five more packs to go."

All through the afternoon we sat in the tent, polishing off the package of Lucky Strikes. That evening we opened a can of beans and ate them cold. There wasn't time for building a fire or setting out a tablecloth, and we took our nourishment directly from the container. When one is embarking on a life of sin, there is no room for observing the niceties.

We slept soundly but woke up with a novel and heretofore unexperienced taste in our mouths. By eight o'clock we were at work again on a pack of Camels. Although we were unable to distinguish the taste of one brand as compared to another, we said we could. At the time, I thought we were smoking, but Bill pointed out around noon that we weren't inhaling the smoke and thus were not taking full advantage of the tar and nicotine.

So, little by little, we began drawing smoke into our lungs, where it would do some good. The effect was delicious. It sent us reeling around the island, laughing and bumping into trees and falling over rocks. Several years later, I was to experience the same sensation from my first martini.

In legend, young people trying the weed for the first time are supposed to become deathly ill after their first crack at the vice. The moral is that the boys learn a good lesson and go on to become Boy Scout leaders and deacons of the church, and to collect for the Red Cross. Somehow, though, this didn't happen to us. We continued to eat our cold beans from the can in a smoky tent and to discuss the ways of the world in a very enlightened fashion.

By the third day we had achieved success. We craved a cigarette about every half hour. We knew how to blow smoke rings. And we developed a nonchalance about the whole business that would have done credit to Shorty Gould.

When the last of the weeds were gone, we made an instant and unanimous decision to return home, where our cigarette supply could be replenished.

We had obtained our objective: we were seasoned young men who knew a thing or two about the world. The principal obstacle now lay in bringing our great discovery into the open, but this turned out to be easier than I would have guessed. While I was getting cleaned up after three days of debauchery on the island, my mother noticed the yellow stains on the fingers of my left hand. She didn't say anything then, but a few minutes later she appeared with a cigarette in her mouth.

"How long have you been doing that?" I asked, shocked.

"Since I was fourteen," she said, flicking the ash expertly. "Only I never smoked in front of you children. Now I won't have to wait until you and Stuart have gone to bed. Here, have one of mine."

I took one and lighted it, and from then on she matched me cigarette for cigarette until she was nearly eighty years old. Then she quit because, as she said, she was afraid she might get the habit.

Bill and I also helped Shorty Gould explode the stunt-your-growth theory. We both topped out at exactly six feet three inches.

chapter six

Learning the Useful Arts

I understand that college students today can earn credits toward a Bachelor's degree by enrolling in a course that teaches the fundamentals of learning to sail a boat. Apparently the course lasts an entire semester, although I don't know how that's possible unless the students actually build the boats.

Back in the dark days of long ago, we had to learn how to sail from our fathers. I remember the brief course mine gave me one summer afternoon.

"Son," he said at lunch, "around two o'clock, I'll knock off work and we'll go down to the river and learn to sail."

The new little boat had been delivered by Cass Adams that morning so there was quite a lot of excitement in the air. Moreover, it was my boat, earned by piloting a hayrake around our fields behind Charley Horse. The bargain between my father and me had been a gentleman's agreement. No documents, just a firm handshake. If I would agree to do the raking, he would ask Cass Adams to build a fourteen-foot sailboat. Both parties had fulfilled their promises; the hay was in the loft and the boat was at the dock.

At two o'clock my father came down to the river and our course began. He helped me raise the spritsail; then he took his place at the rudder. I cast off the dock line. "Now, son," he said, "pay attention. If you push the tiller away from you, the boat will turn in the opposite direction. Like this." He demonstrated this maneuver a couple of times, and I caught on right away. "On the other hand," he continued, "if you pull the tiller toward you, the bow turns away. Get it?" I said I did. "Good," he said. "Now we'll tack over to Jackson's Landing."

This was about a hundred yards away, and the new boat beat smartly up the river until we were opposite Professor Jackson's dock. "Ready about," my father cried, and we went over on the other tack and picked up speed. But just before we ran into the marsh grass off Shankhassick Point, my father whipped the tiller around and headed the bow for home. He let out the sheet and we skimmed along. "This is running before the wind," he said. "Just remember to keep the boom out of the water."

Back at our dock, he brought the bow into the wind and laid the boat alongside. As soon as I had made fast, he stepped ashore and gazed down at the trim little vessel. "Now you know how to sail, son," he said. "I hope you'll always enjoy it." With that, he strode up the dock and headed for his typewriter.

The time was fifteen minutes past two o'clock. I am at a loss to understand how modern educators can stretch this course into several months.

Learning to drive a car was different. This required enormous amounts of practice in a field close to the river. The vehicle was a 1920 Chevrolet touring car, and it proved to be quite an attention-getter.

By the time Stu and I were thirteen we were accomplished masters of the internal-combustion engine. My father didn't even bother to give us any lessons in the art of handling an automobile, and there was no driver-training course in the Durham school. It was every kid for himself in 1923. We simply pushed in the clutch, yanked the gear lever into low, and steered toward the open field. Here we circled around and made figure eights and pretended we were Barney Oldfield. All in low gear.

After a bit, this became old hat to both of us, but not to an Irish terrier named Bridget, whose usual place in this self-training program was on the front seat between us. She enjoyed the companionship and she liked the motion of the car as it bumped around the field. In fact, she became something of an addict to gasoline power.

The Chevrolet had running boards. These were an uncommonly useful part of those old cars and served as a step for the driver as he dismounted from his perch. Later they were to go out of style as automobile manufacturers developed newer models that could bang your head and wallop your knee in one smooth motion.

The running boards on the Chevy added a good deal to our enjoyment of the new pastime. We could stand on them and steer the vehicle from the outside. You can't do that with today's cars.

Because our field excursions were conducted in low gear, we sometimes were able, for novelty's sake, to jump off and trot alongside. Thus we were able to view objectively the dog alone on the front seat. Furthermore, Bridget's anxiousness to please made it possible for us to place her front paws on the steering wheel. She made an enchanting picture, not unlike the illustrations in a book we were reading, called *Wind in the Willows*. Toad drove an automobile. Well, so did our Bridget.

Directly across from our practice field was a highway leading from the seacoast to the state capital. In those days it was simply called the Dover Road. And not very good at that. Nowadays it is known as U.S. 4, complete with a by-pass, traffic lights, and a lurking state trooper. But in 1923 a motorist could look across the narrow part of the Oyster River and watch two kids and a dog and a Chevrolet with its top down driving slowly across our field.

This was novel but not quite good enough, because of the Chevy's natural inclination to move straight ahead toward the river or into a ditch. A piece of clothesline did the trick. By cramping the steering wheel hard over, and holding it fast with the clothesline, we could make the car move in a circle endlessly, or until the gasoline tank ran dry.

Prior to this discovery, viewers from the Dover Road had merely seen two youngsters running alongside the car while an Irish terrier steered. Now they were treated to quite an eye-popping spectacle. While Stu and I hid behind the stone wall, Bridget sat happily upright on the front seat with her paws on the wheel, her ears pointing jauntily forward, and her tongue out. To the two of us, this was the greatest thing since the day we found a dead cow in Tony Morse's well.

The public reaction to all this was not fully appreciated until some time later. My father was informed of it late one afternoon by a motorist who came roaring down the driveway and began banging at the front door. When my father opened it, he was confronted by a man, considerably agitated, who managed to blurt out, "Th-th-there's a dog driving a car around your field, mister!"

My father was startled for a moment, but then he resumed his normal calm, and accompanied the bearer of the news toward the barn, where they could get a better look at the field. The motorist pointed to the revolving Chevrolet and Bridget, and stuttered some more. "See, right there — th-th-that *dog* is driving your car!"

Taking in the scene at a glance, my father came to the correct conclusion. Turning to the motorist, he shook his fist in the direction of the field and declared, "I told that dog not to take the car out again by herself. I can't seem to make her mind!"

While the motorist made odd noises in his throat, my father thanked him for reporting Bridget's deceitful ways and returned to the house.

Afterward, my father told the story to Charlie Wentworth, and Sam Runlett, and Frank Morrison. When he came to describing the look on the motorist's face at the point in the tale where he shook his fist at the dog, he would have to sit down and get his breath. The tears would roll right down his cheeks.

Charlie and Frank and Sam embellished the story in later years. The last time I heard it, Stuart and I had actually taught Bridget to drive a Chevrolet, and the only thing that kept her from going into town for the mail was New Hampshire's obstinate refusal to issue driving licenses to dogs.

chapter seven

Earn Big Money at Home

IN the early twenties, the country's largest fur mart was located in Saint Louis, and one of its principal activities was sending out price lists to small boys. This was its own fault. The companies advertised themselves as huge purchasers of raw pelts at the highest prices. "Send for Our Price List Today."

Most of us did. Each boy would fill in the coupon at the bottom of the advertisement, and presently another letter from Saint Louis was waiting for him in the mailbox. Thus we were able to make comparisons between the many firms and ascertain for ourselves exactly where we could obtain the most money for the skins of the fox, lynx, bear, mink, and otter that we were going to trap. Obviously, this was as good as accomplished because the advertisement said it was. "Turn Your Spare Time into Money by Trapping," one of them tempted us. Another stated categorically, "There's Good Money To Be Made Right on Your Own Farm with a Dozen Grip-Tight Traps."

The prices made heady reading. A silver fox was listed as being worth five hundred to two thousand dollars.

My favorite company was the Eagle Fur Company, located at Main and Market in Saint Louis. It recognized a zealous trapper when it heard from one, for in addition to the price list it enclosed a shipping tag that bore its modest slogan, "Above All." On the back side of the tag, the company sent a message directly to me. "CONFIDENCE," it stated, "MEANS MUCH TO FUR SHIPPERS." Then it told me why. "Eagle Fur Co. shippers have confidence because they always receive quick returns and top market prices without one cent deducted for commission. These are the facts and if you are not an Eagle fur shipper get busy and use this tag on your next shipment and be convinced. Once a shipper always a shipper to EAGLE FUR CO., St. Louis, Mo., U.S.A. ABOVE ALL."

Right away, the Eagle Fur Company had established itself as a reliable firm to which I could ship my pelts with confidence. Obviously I could look forward to a long and mutually profitable association with these gentlemen.

For Christmas that year I asked for and received a dozen steel fox traps. They were menacing objects with serrated jaws, and the springs were strong enough to snap a piece of kindling into bits. I tried them out on the hearth that morning, after opening my other presents, and my mother was so appalled that she made me take them out to the woodshed.

I would have done this anyway because I had just read three or four books about trappers around Hudson Bay, and I had learned that the one thing a fox doesn't care for is a trap all covered with human scent. The really successful trappers who brought their furs into the Hudson Bay posts generally smoked their traps over fires before setting out their lines. This killed the scent, and the fox thought he was just running over an old campfire. That's the way the half-Cree Indians did it, and that was good enough for me.

Just outside the woodshed door, I kindled a small fire and dangled my traps over it until they were black. After that, I only handled them with gloves that had been smeared with bacon grease. Bear grease would have been better, but at the time I didn't have a bear handy.

That afternoon, working on snowshoes and loaded down with the smoked traps, I ran my line. Every known art of the wilds was employed in making my sets. Pieces of Christmas turkey were hung from brush above the traps. And when these had been set I covered them with snow and brushed the area lightly with a pine bough. I had read enough about half-Cree Indians to understand the value of this. The fox, unaware that a small boy was after him, would smell the turkey, scout the area, and seeing no signs of danger other than some snow brushed lightly by a pine bough, would step onto the trigger of my trap. From there it was but a short step to the Eagle Fur Company in Saint Louis, where my confidence lay.

Unfortunately, more snow fell that night, but this did not bother me much. I could remember the location of each trap, and besides, there were going to be twelve foxes thrashing around anyway.

By noontime I had found the traps by poking around in the new snow with a stick. This caused them to spring, of course, and it was cold work resetting them in a foot of snow. This was a far cry from the impression that I had received from the Hudson Bay books. In these, Emil LeTouch snow-shoed tirelessly twenty or thirty miles a day, collecting his pelts, munching his pemmican, and singing happily in broken English about his li'l papoose and its mother.

Not one of those books said anything about the virtually impossible task of resetting a fox trap in a foot of snow. They hadn't been difficult to set on the woodshed floor, which was hard and level, because I could get a foot on each spring to compress it before performing the delicate business of engaging the trigger. But it was a different story out in the wilds.

In order to step on the springs, I had to take off my snow-shoes and stand them up. Then I had to dig down to bare ground so I would have something solid on which to compress the springs. Finally, working with heavy, bacon-smeared mittens, I had to reach between the jaws of the trap and fool around with the trigger mechanism. By the time all this was accomplished, my fingers were numb from the cold, my feet were half frozen, and I could understand why the Eagle Fur Company was willing to pay up to two thousand dollars for one fox pelt. Nor did I croon any song about the li'l papoose and Marie, or munch pemmican. Instead, I cussed. I cussed out the fox, the traps, the Eagle Fur Company of Saint Louis, and the profit motive. And after I finally had a trap set and properly anchored to a piece of brush, and the bait in place, the whole arena looked as though two buffalo had fought a duel in the vicinity. No fox in his right mind would have come near the place.

In less than two weeks my fox-trapping phase was finished, despite continuing pleas from the Eagle Fur Company to ship with confidence. I collected my traps and traded them to Lawrence Page for a home course in taxidermy. He had paid twelve dollars to some mail-order professor of taxidermy for an instruction book on the art of stuffing wild birds and animals. Like me, he had been lured by advertisements in sporting magazines to "Earn Big Money at Home." When the book arrived, he went through it pretty rapidly, and then he shot a bluejay. During all his spare time from school and chores for a period of one week, he tried to stuff that bird by following the directions from the professor.

When he finished, he had something that looked as though it had spent a couple of nights in a saloon. One glassy eye stared straight up into the sky, and the other peered at its own dangling legs. The left wing wouldn't lie flat and the right wing drooped on the table. Lawrence said he hadn't got the wire in right, but he guessed he wouldn't fix it because he would have had to unsew the bird and remove the stuffing. Furthermore, the young taxidermist must have skipped a lesson or two about preparing the bird for its debut into polite society. This bluejay was powerful even in the woodshed.

We both came away from the swapping session satisfied. Lawrence had a new trade, and I was about to embark on a life's career. That evening, I raced through the professor's course in record time. It was easy to see where Lawrence had gone wrong. He had failed to send for the special instruments required by the art. These cost nineteen dollars and ninety-five cents, plus postage, and according to the professor they were the keys to a lucrative profession.

As it happened, I had nineteen dollars and ninety-five cents; various aunts and uncles had given me money for Christmas. But I was still young enough to require parental consent before I could spend it. So that night I brought the professor's book to the dinner table to prove my case. I explained that I had decided to become the world's greatest taxidermist. In order to accomplish this, I was in need of the proper tools.

"What are they?" my father asked.

"Well, there's quite a list of things," I replied. "There's the preservative for the skin, and a scalpel, and special scissors, and wire, and stuffing material, and glass eyes, and a brain spoon."

"A what?" my father exclaimed.

"A brain spoon," I said. "You have to spoon out the bird's brain before you push the skull back into the skin. Lawrence Page didn't do that, and his bluejay smells awful."

"That will do, son," my father said. "We'll talk about it after we've finished eating." He had glanced at my mother, who was looking a little pale.

But after dinner, we did get back to brain spoons in the living room. "It's your money, son," my father said. "If you want to spend it on this set and become the greatest taxidermist in the world, go ahead. I suggest that you carry out your operations in the woodshed or the barn, so your mother won't see them."

So the next day I sent to the professor for the kit and settled down to becoming the most famous taxidermist of the 1900s. When it arrived, I tried it out on a gray squirrel.

Within a couple of days I discovered that some people have the knack of stuffing wild animals, and some don't. I didn't. When it came time in the process to take up the brain spoon, I gagged. Finally, I threw the mangled remains over a stone wall, closed my office, and took down my sign. The greatest taxidermist of the day was through.

I passed the torch along to Tater Watson, together with the tools of the trade, and received in return an air-pump BB gun which could set a horse or cow in motion at a distance of fifty feet. It was my judgment at the time that a well-oiled, properly aimed BB gun offered more genuine entertainment than twelve traps or a brain spoon. I still think so, but our no-nonsense state legislature made BB guns illegal a few years ago.

chapter eight

Down on Their Luck

ONE summer my father bought a deserted farm diagonally across the river from our own place. It consisted of twenty-five acres, in the center of which were a livable house, a small barn, and a chicken coop. The view down the river was superb. However, the place was chiefly noted for its succession of tenants who for the moment were down on their luck. They weren't underprivileged or even poor. They were simply down and out, which was a good New Hampshire expression in those days.

My father had a way of collecting these unfortunates and moving them into the house across the river until their luck changed. Usually a cow and some hens went along with the farm, as well as a hired man's job here at Shankhassick. Then, when things got better, the head of the household would hanker for something new and move on. It was my father's private rehabilitation center, as well as his hobby, and before long another down-on-their-luck family would be living in the house across the river.

There were two families that I remember best. One was the Bergerons, who were French Canadians. The father, Bill, was a wood chopper. He and his large family occupied a tarpaper shack on the Newmarket Road, but about two weeks before one Christmas, his ax slipped and he cut a gash halfway through his foot. The outlook for Christmas was dark indeed until my father stopped by Runlett's store on Christmas Eve for some groceries. He overheard Sam telling a customer about the dim prospects at the Bergeron household with no money and a meager supply of food, and Bill lying in bed with a festering wound. My father almost swept the shelves of Runlett's store bare. There were sacks of flour and potatoes and sugar. And milk and meat and a turkey. Another box was jammed with toys for the kids.

Until he strode through the door of the wretched shack that night he had never seen the Bergerons, and they had never laid eyes on him. But he must have been an answer to a prayer. Suddenly there was ample food, with Doctor Grant treating the infected foot, and the promise of a job as soon as the foot mended, and of course the house and farm across the river.

The Bergerons moved in a few weeks later and remained for three years. Every morning Bill would come across the river on the ice, or he would row over in a boat, and cut wood and do chores. He was as strong as an ox, and to prove it to us youngsters, he would sometimes get under the pony's belly and lift him off the ground. His every remark was begun with "Py chee." "Py chee, she's gonna rain today. I seen de t'underbirds." None of us ever saw the t'underbirds, but Bill did, and generally he was right about the rain.

Toward the end of the three years, Bill began to show signs of wanting to move on, and for a number of weeks he indicated this by failing to turn up on Monday mornings. My father suspected that these illnesses were being caused by too much homemade wine on Sundays so he confronted Bill with his suspicions. Bill was outraged. "Py chee, Mr. Paine. One leetle cup. Dat's all. Just one leetle cup for de healt'." But then he started to miss Tuesdays as well. At that, my father had another talk with him, and Bill confessed he was feeling restless. The parting was amicable, with a profusion of "t'anks" to my father for coming to their rescue when they were down and out.

After they left, several other families enjoyed the farm; then along came the Smiths (as I shall call them). Mrs. Smith produced children at about the same rate as a cow, and Mr. Smith was hard put to feed the growing herd on a janitor's salary. So they moved in.

With them came a son we called Reddy at school, and he was no genius. I once hit him on the head with a baseball bat over by the teeter boards for stealing three marbles from me. He barely glanced up. Whether this incident had anything to do with his later accomplishments, I have no way of knowing. But a couple of years after that, a whole lot of grass fires broke out on the farm across the river where the Smiths were living. It seemed as though we owned the most inflammable grass in the whole town. There were twenty of these little blazes during an interval of three weeks.

Then one Saturday night, the chicken coop went up in flames from spontaneous combustion. That's what the fire department experts said it was, anyway. From our side of the river, it made quite a sight.

A week later, the fire whistle blew again, and we all looked across the river while the barn burned down from spontaneous combustion. By this time, there were certain suspicions being formed that spontaneous combustion was extraordinarily active at the Smith place. But before anybody got around to doing something about it, the whistle blew again on a Saturday night, and we watched as the house across the river went up in smoke.

There was evidence to indicate that Reddy was overly fascinated by matches and kerosene, and eventually he was sent to the reform school, as it was called in those days. I believe the state is still supporting him at some higher-level institution, but under confinement now.

But that ended my father's own personal rehabilitation center. As far as the Bergerons and the Smiths were concerned, the score came out about fifty-fifty. The Bergeron family left in their automobile, nicely dressed and completely restored. One son went to Cornell and now owns a tree-surgery company. The Smiths, on the other hand, left without their clothes, their car, their furniture . . . and their thick-skulled son, Reddy.

chapter nine

A Dam Goot Cabin

Besides leaving us with words that enriched our vocabularies, Bill Bergeron left behind a monument that still stands as straight and true as it did when he uttered his last "Py chee, she's a dam goot cabin." That was fifty-five years ago.

I don't remember who it was that suggested the log cabin by the river. Perhaps it was Bill himself. He had a way of going into the woods and flailing around with his ax until an area looked like the pictures of France during World War I. There were no robins in the hair of any tree Bill saw. Trees from his standpoint were put there for only one reason: to be chopped down. Or my father may have suggested the log cabin after Bill had devastated forty or fifty pine trees down by the spring.

Whoever made the first move, we were all suddenly plunged into the construction of a new and exciting enterprise. We would have our own camp, py chee. The previous summer, we had been lugged off to a cottage twenty miles away for the month of August. At the end of the first week, my father gave up and came back to the farm. After the second week, my brother and I found so little to do that we asked to return to salt water. So my mother packed our things and

61

turned the cottage over to a young couple who happened to come along.

But our own log cabin would be different. Although the proposed site could easily be seen from the house, it was remote enough to let us believe it was out in the wilds. Everybody took a hand in its planning, including Bill, who had probably built a score of cabins during his lifetime. Nothing was put on paper. As he had done with the ells and additions that had gradually been tacked onto the main house, my father simply made some marks in the field with his heel, and these represented the dimensions. They turned out to be eighteen feet by fourteen feet, which was what an architect likely would have suggested anyway.

Therewith, Bill spat on his hands, sharpened his ax, and disappeared into the woods. We saw him at night when he returned to go down to his boat to row home, and again in the morning when I turned the grindstone for him. The one thing a wood chopper in those days wouldn't tolerate was a dull tool. Under his tutelage, I got to be a pretty fair grindstone-turner. "A leetle more slow," Bill would say. Or, "A leetle more fast, boy." This was when I was beginning to get tired. Then he would try out the edge on the hair of his arm, and if the black bristles came off cleanly, he would say, "Py chee, she's goot."

Grindstone-turners of that day got through their tasks by thinking about more pleasant things. At best, it was a tiresome job, making a wheel go around and around. But Bill helped enliven the morning drudgery by recounting stories of his lumber-camp life, and the number of cords of wood he had cut in a fifteen-hour day. It was prodigious. He also had a good deal to say about eels, which he caught in the river at night. A lot of these he brought over to give to Violet, who didn't like the way they squirmed in the pan after they had been cut into sections. But on the table they were delicious.

As soon as he had slaughtered what he considered a proper number of pine trees for a cabin, Bill harnessed Charley Horse and snaked the trees out of the woods and down to the site. Then he showed us how to peel the bark from a pine log. He could do some miraculous things with his ax. At a speed that was hard to keep up with, he slit the pine bark from end to end and deftly undressed the tree. Stu and I never got the knack; probably our hatchets weren't sharp enough. But our handiwork is still there. We used drawshaves, and the logs that look as though they had spent a winter with the beavers still stand out from those Bill peeled.

There has always been some good-natured contention over who really did build the cabin. Our older brother Del sometimes maintains that he was only thirteen when he and Bill heaved the logs into position and spiked them to the corner uprights. That would have made Stu and me eight years old. If Del is right, the shingling job that lasted until 1941 was a pretty good one for boys of that age. Actually, we twins were ten and Del was fifteen. But the question is academic anyway. Bill Bergeron built the cabin, all the while having to put up with three bothersome helpers.

When the cabin was finished, we decided that everybody in the family would move down to the river for the rest of the summer. We kids thought that was a great idea, but why our parents were willing to leave running water and a comfortable house in order to sleep on cots and walk two hundred yards to a privy was a mystery.

It took a bit of doing. We seldom went into such things easily, and this time a whole new household had to be set up within sight of a perfectly good home. There were cots and blankets, and kerosene lamps and a three-burner kerosene stove. An old milk-cooler was converted into a water tank that could be hauled to the house every second day for replenishing. Chairs and tables were rummaged from the attic. A set of china was broken out of a barrel where it had been stored for eighteen years, and was arranged on shelves at the cabin. A box of cooking utensils was scooped up from the kitchen of the house. At this, Violet asked for a week's vacation and left for Canada.

Bill Bergeron, on the other hand, was proud of his handiwork. "Py chee, dat one fine cabin." He built a platform behind it and erected a tent. This would be sleeping quarters for my brothers and me. Our father and mother were to sleep on the screened porch.

When everybody had lugged as much stuff as he could think of to our new home, we closed the doors to the house and trooped to the cabin for the night. It was a smashing success. Even though we could see the house when we woke up and peered through the tent flaps, we felt that we had moved a thousand miles away.

Of course, the grownups went through their usual tasks during the day. My father walked to his shop, and my mother usually went up to putter in her gardens. By suppertime, however, we all returned to the lives of frontiersmen down by the river.

The remarkable aspect of this return to nature was that it lasted a month. When Violet returned from Canada to see if any of us could be reasoned with, she found herself the sole occupant of the house. When friends of my parents dropped by, Violet would roll her eyes toward the river and direct the visitors, "Follow those tracks and you can't miss them." Then she would shrug her shoulders to indicate her opinion of our sanity.

Daft or not, a surprising number of similar cabins were erected along the river the following summer.

Bill's cabin was to play an even more remarkable role three years later. It became a honeymoon cottage. When my Aunt Elizabeth wrote from New York that she had been married, my mother offered her and her new husband the cabin for the summer. There was nothing unusual about my aunt's getting married. People did that all the time. What made it a little bizarre was that she was fifty-two years old while the groom was twenty-six. Moreover, he was an artist. If this weren't scary enough, he was an Italian artist who had left Rome only six months before. His English, she had written, was not yet perfect.

Aunt Elizabeth wasn't like most people. She ran a settlement house in New York City. She believed in Causes. Her conversations were generally a mixture of radical ideas: immigrants were human, women should vote, Standard Oil was a monster. Now she had married an Italian immigrant, half her age, who painted. All this promised an interesting summer.

"Thank God for the cabin," my mother said. She and Aunt Elizabeth were able to keep a line of communication open for approximately twenty-four hours. After that, it became worn. Although my mother's opinions on immigrants, the ladies' vote, and Standard Oil were similar, she didn't see why Aunt Elizabeth had to keep talking about them all the time.

Such an ado there was about readying the cabin for the bridal couple! Curtains were draped at the windows. Screens were added. The stove was overhauled. Shelves were built to hold the tiers of canned goods, for it was correctly judged that an Italian artist only just arrived on these shores might require some help with the provisions.

The discrepancy in their ages was more striking than my aunt's letter had admitted. Pietro had a great mop of black hair, huge shoulders, extraordinarily white teeth, and a laugh that was really a roar. Aunt Elizabeth, on the other hand, looked exactly fifty-two: gray haired, worried about money, and determined to make us like her immigrant if it killed us.

She was right to worry about how she was going to support him, but she needn't have bothered her head about our liking Pete. We all did. He was far closer in age to us boys than he was to his new wife. When we went swimming, he not only beat us but kept on swimming for a mile or two more. He quickly caught on to American baseball, and could likewise trounce us at our own game.

Moreover, he could paint. He would sit out in the field, stripped to the waist, and work at a canvas every morning. Then he would bring it to the cabin and boom, "I deed it myself." That got to be quite an expression around here for a while. Occasionally, he would switch to portrait painting, and all of us took turns being his subject.

If Aunt Elizabeth had had any notion that she and Pete were going to spend a sequestered honeymoon in New Hampshire, she must have been disappointed. The waterfront was our natural habitat during the summer, and we saw no reason to change it because they were living there. Furthermore, her immigrant was the hero of our swimming clique.

Pietro also introduced a new style of dress to Durham. For the first time, a grown male was observed on Main Street wearing nothing but a pair of bathing trunks. The Italians must have been about two decades ahead of us in this respect — or Pietro was, for he often swam the half-mile to Hamilton Smith's boathouse and then walked into the center of the village. This innovation set the ladies clacking, you may be sure of that. Many years passed before another pair of bathing trunks with a man in it was seen on Main Street.

It was pretty tame around here after Aunt Elizabeth and her Pietro returned to New York in the fall. There was no half-naked Italian sketching in the field anymore. The great swimming meets were over. We still exclaimed "I deed it myself" when the occasion arose, but it wasn't the real thing. We missed Pete. But the true virtue of the cabin had been demonstrated. My mother and Aunt Elizabeth had passed three months within a quarter of a mile of each other without once mentioning the sins of Standard Oil.

And that was progress, py chee.

chapter ten

Fooling the Tax Man

Thete were several days one year when we thought that my father was going to be put in jail.

"Anyway," he told my mother one evening, "I should be able to get a lot of writing done. Not many interruptions, and jails are notoriously quiet. The food is simple but filling. And nothing to do but pound away at the typewriter. I guess it won't be so bad at that."

A call from the Internal Revenue Service, asking to see him about something in his previous year's income tax, had sent him into a tailspin. For a man who had been a war correspondent and a reporter in New York City he was curiously naive about this newfangled Federal bureau. Furthermore, the amount was little more than one hundred dollars. Not the amount in dispute either; that was the entire tax. Calvin Coolidge was still keeping a thrifty eye on the treasury.

When the agent called a second time and asked for a definite appointment, my father began to take evasive action. He had agreed to meet the Federal sleuth at the railroad station and bring him down to the farm. The IRS at that time had not realized its full potential for harassing citizens, and it did

69

not supply its agents with cars. The suspected culprit was expected to furnish the local transportation.

However, this fitted perfectly into my father's scheme. The year before had been a good one for him. Royalty checks had arrived at the mailbox in satisfactory amounts to keep everything humming around here. We had become a two-car family. There was the eight-year-old open job that was used for errands, and right beside it was a shiny new model called a demi-sedan. Like most people then and now, Father's attitude toward tax assessors and tax collectors was defensive. The new car might appear to the agent, he thought, as plain evidence that there must have been chicanery on the tax form. So he planned to take it down to the cabin and park it behind some trees. Then at the appointed hour, he would drive the older and somewhat battered car to the station. This was intended to indicate to the revenue man that he was dealing with a man whose previous year's income had been barely above the subsistence level.

He had other schemes, too. For a while, he toyed with the notion of driving the agent to a deserted house farther down Durham Point Road, where my mother would pretend that she was in the final throes of her last illness, but he abandoned that as too far-fetched. However, he discussed the subject of clothes for quite a while. He wanted himself and the whole family to look shabby when the tax man arrived. For us kids that was not too difficult — we weren't called the mud rats for nothing. But for my father it was impossible. Summer and winter, he did his writing dressed in a stiff collar, a tie, and a coat. It was not unusual to see him hoeing the garden late in the afternoon wearing a Panama hat above the traditional collar and tie. So he switched to planning a suitable location for the meeting.

He ruled out the house because it was filled with old furniture that might be taken for antiques. Moreover, the Oriental rugs looked expensive. His workshop, on the other hand, was crammed with knickknacks he had collected while a war correspondent, as well as books. These last he could explain away as part of his trade, and the swords and guns were souvenirs of the Spanish-American War. Thus he finally settled on his workshop as the ideal spot for the great inquest.

But he continued to worry. Despite my mother's repeated assurances that no one would be faced with a long jail sentence just because he had made a little mistake on his income-tax form, he continued to talk about dungeons and prisons and wardens at every meal. It worried us kids, too.

When finally the afternoon arrived for the tax man to appear at the station, my father took the new car down to the river and hid it behind some trees, just as he had so craftily planned. Then he went off to meet the two-o'clock train from Dover. When he reappeared in the driveway, he was accompanied by a sleek young man, the forerunner of the thousands of sleek young men who were eventually to swarm over the country like locusts. My father and he went to the workshop, the agent carrying under his arm a briefcase that was uncommonly large for those days. We decided it must contain a detailed dossier on my father's short, unhappy association with the Internal Revenue Service.

The shop was about a hundred feet from the house, so Stu and I hung around, pretending to be clipping the grass and weeding the gardens. Presently we heard laughter coming from the workshop. In a few more minutes, the two of them came through the door and settled themselves on a settee my father kept on the porch. Here the conversation continued for another hour, and we could catch snatches of it from our listening posts. "Sure, I knew Richard Harding Davis," my father said. "A great reporter. But Stephen Crane was the one I enjoyed the most. Once in Florida, he and I . . . ." Here my father lowered his voice, and we failed to catch what had happened in Florida to Stephen Crane and himself. But from the tone of the conversation, we could tell that our father probably was not going to be hauled off to jail that afternoon, so we went back to constructing a new mast for the boat. By the time we were through, the agent and my father had left for the railroad station.

When he returned we rushed up to the car, and my mother came out the door.

"What did he want?" we asked in unison.

"He wants to be a writer," my father said in that particular tone he used for people who came to him asking for literary advice. But we could see that he was relieved.

"What about the income tax?" my mother asked.

"Oh, that," he said. "A one looked like a seven. He couldn't make out which. It was just an excuse. He had his briefcase stuffed full of books, and he asked me to autograph them for him. That was about it."

"What did you tell him about writing?"

"Everything I know about it," my father said.

"What's that?" I asked.

"*Write*," replied my father, getting out of the car.

My mother teased him for a while about all his worrying beforehand, but he took it good-naturedly. It wasn't until he announced in some panic after dinner that the new car had been stolen that we knew how really worried he had been.

chapter eleven

Running Water

IN the summer of 1909 my family abandoned "Wellville" and moved indoors. (Wellville was the name of the privy that had served them up to that time.) The move was possible because gasoline power had caught on in Durham, and water no longer had to be pumped by hand.

Pipe was laid to a rainwater cistern a few feet from the house, and Thirty-Seven-Fifty was installed in the cellar, with a long exhaust pipe running through the wall to the outdoors. The engine got its name because that was what it cost, retail. It ran a pump that pushed the cistern water up to the attic and into a zinc-lined tank; additional plumbing brought the water down again to a bathroom on the first floor, and presto! The greatest advance in human living standards since man first stretched out for the night in a cave had been accomplished. The path to Wellville was gradually taken over by brush until no trace of it could be seen. But the building was kept painted and shingled until 1939.

Thirty-Seven-Fifty performed faithfully until 1916. However, as more bathrooms were added, the sturdy little engine was hard put to meet the demand. Furthermore, during dry spells the cistern was equally hard pressed to sustain three bathrooms. And we were still hauling our drinking water by hand from a clear, cold spring more than a fifth of a mile from the house.

By 1916, the single-cylinder engine, customarily known as the "one-lunger," was being treated with new respect. Little Thirty-Seven-Fifty had proved that the make-and-break system of ignition was no longer the concept of a demented mind. It worked. Moreover, with minor adjustments, generally accomplished with a sledgehammer and a Jesus wrench, it could be made to go on working for extended periods of time. Make-and-break ignition likewise spruced up the English language with a totally new arrangement of sacred words. Any accomplishment I have today in this art can be traced back to those years when I listened to plumbers and mechanics talk to one-lung engines. I don't know anybody now who talks to engines, but in those days, dialogue was an essential ingredient of the mechanic's trade.

One-lungers were better than any other form of power then available in the countryside. They beat the horse by a mile because they didn't eat when they weren't working. They were superior to pumping by hand, even though the starting process often used up more energy than would otherwise have been expended on the pump handle. Also, one-lungers held men spellbound wherever one of the things could be made to run. Males would sit and sniff its heady fumes and stare at the revolving flywheel by the hour.

With the cistern failing to keep pace with the bathrooms, my father decided to pipe water in from the spring that was our drinking supply. This was not something to be undertaken lightly. It required a thousand feet of ditch digging, blasting through ledge, and the installation of a windmill near the spring and of a huge tank on the hill overlooking the house.

Two ditch-diggers who were known only as "the Italians" settled down for the summer and began wielding their picks and shovels. They worked nine hours a day, six days a week, for twelve dollars a week. First they dug the trench to the house. That required two months. Then they set out on a quest for the windmill site. They burrowed off in a southerly direction for a couple of hundred feet, only to discover when they got there that the surrounding trees made the proposed location a veritable vacuum. On the windiest days, not even the slightest breeze disturbed the tranquillity of this sequestered place. So they spat on their hands and burrowed off in another direction for three hundred feet, throwing the clay up and out of the ditch with tireless efficiency. This spot made the first one look like a hurricane in full force. Birds had trouble flying over it, the air was so still. Butterflies fell to the ground for lack of draft. In half a gale, matches could be lighted at this windmill site, and they would burn slowly down to their ends without flickering.

Although the windmill had already been delivered, in various boxes and crates, it was put into a shed and abandoned.

E.A. Prescott now entered the fray. He was the plumber, and his ability to talk to pumps and one-lung engines was legendary. He treated them as brothers, but he wasn't above occasionally fetching them a sound smack with a crowbar. His solution to the windmill problem was to replace it with a magnificent red make-and-break engine that weighed five hundred pounds and was certified to deliver five horsepower.

This staggering amount of power was transferred by belt to a big double-action pump manufactured by Lunt Moss in Boston. Later on, this name nearly drove everybody crazy because the pump — though located a thousand feet away — made all the pipes in the cellar groan and wheeze. And the thing they wheezed so rhythmically was *Lunt ... Moss, Lunt ... Moss.* Five or six hours at a time.

Mr. Prescott likewise erected a water tower on the top of a hill near the house. It soared sixty feet into the air, and the tank could be seen for several miles. Municipal water systems used larger tanks, but not much. This one was designed to hold enough water to keep the household going for a full week, and even Lunt Moss required eight hours to fill it, wheeze and all.

After Mr. Prescott had spoken a few words to the engine, he laid to with the crank and got the big flywheels turning over. Then he said a few other things and turned on the ignition. He was rewarded with a stupendous bark from the exhaust pipe, then another and another. It was running on its own power now, and presently the pump picked up its prime and the new water system was in operation. The Italians filled in the ditch to the house and the one that had been dug to the second windmill site, and departed. The first windmill ditch is still there, a sort of inverted monument to the two earth-movers from across the sea.

I wish I could report that Mr. Prescott's sensational hydro-gasoline system solved all our water problems forever and ever. It didn't. The principal drawback, soon to become apparent, was that the weekly skirmishes with the engine were now carried on a fifth of a mile from the house instead of in the cellar.

Every nut, bolt, washer, wrench, quart of oil, gallon of gasoline, or replacement belt had to be lugged a thousand feet along a path through pine woods. On good days, when the engine had been properly spoken to beforehand, only three or four trips were necessary to rouse the great red beast. But when its mood was uncertain and balky, twenty visits were often required. For one thing, the hopeful operator had to come up the path occasionally for nourishment. Frequently the tussles lasted all day, and then some. Lanterns would burn until late in the evening.

A building known as the Spring House was erected around and over the battleground, and, as the years passed, it became filled with an assortment of oil cans, broken wrenches, discarded belts, human skin, and a good many internal organs of the five-horsepower manic depressive and old Lunt Moss itself.

The new water tower likewise proved to be temperamental. Because of its height, there was no noticeable difference in our water pressure between high and low tide. It might be filled to the brim with five thousand gallons, or it might have only a few gallons left in the standpipe — the flow from the faucet was the same at the house. We might be brushing our teeth or taking a bath, secure in the belief that all was well, when suddenly there wasn't any water. That signaled the beginning of another round at the Spring House.

During one of these, I got to tell my first big lie. It was a cold morning in December, and the household had awakened to empty pipes. After a meeting only slightly less solemn than the Geneva Convention, I was selected to go forth to the

Spring House and tackle the monster.

I did all the usual things. I primed the pump from a pail that was kept hanging just under the spring cover. Then I coaxed the engine with some pretty fancy English, surprising for a lad of ten, and inserted the crank on the flywheel shaft. With both hands, I got the wheels turning over slowly, and I was about to speak directly to the engine when the crank just slipped from its ratchets. It and I traveled a short distance in a sort of semicircle and came to rest on one of the oil-stained timbers that supported the machine. My knuckles made contact first, and subsequently my head.

After picking myself up, I addressed the engine in the most forthright fashion I could think of. Then I did it. I caught that foolish, no-good mechanical monstrosity a blow to the chin, or in this case the cylinder, with the crank. Imagine my gratification to see a chunk of metal as large as my hand separate from the cylinder and fetch up with a chunk on the other side of the Spring House. Almost immediately, however, my feelings changed from delight to anxiety. It was one thing to see E.A. Prescott kicking the engine base, but quite another for a ten-year-old kid to crack fifteen square inches off its single cylinder. Three inches of the piston lay exposed through the jagged wound.

I retrieved the broken piece and placed it just below the flywheel so that it looked as though it had been blown off, a victim of old age or the croup. That was going to be my lie. It had just broken off when the engine started. But to make that effective I had to start the engine. So I applied the crank again, and after three full turns, there was a blast from the engine pipe. Water once again flowed through the pipes.

When I got back to the house in time for breakfast, I had quite a tale to tell. Nobody doubted my story. My knuckles attested to the skirmish, and so far as I know, no one ever suspected that I had been able to smack that engine hard enough to break off a piece of cast iron almost three-quarters of an inch thick. Not only did the engine run better thereafter but it proved to me the virtue of a judicious lie at the right time.

But that wasn't the end of E.A. Prescott's mechanical marvel, although Mr. Prescott himself came to an end about that time. He was supplanted by a Mr. Simpson, who didn't talk to engines. In fact, Mr. Simpson seldom talked to anybody, an unusual handicap in the plumbing business.

Well, the Silent One took a look at Mr. Prescott's lash-up and decided that the era of the one-lunger was coming to a close. Electricity was the new power, and it was due to arrive at the house. When it finally did, Mr. Simpson suggested that four wires be strung on trees through the woods, and after that he would produce the truly modern miracle. The electric motor.

It was kind of clever the way he did it. First he set a two-horsepower unit on a shelf above the pump and ran a belt to the flywheel of the now-pistonless engine. From there, he ran another belt off the smaller drive hub of the red devil to Lunt Moss itself. He didn't say in so many words that he was trying to "gear it down," but that was the idea. There was one small disadvantage, however, that he had failed to foresee: big fly-wheels had to be set in motion by the familiar crank before the motor switch could be thrown in. Otherwise the new power would simply sizzle and smoke on its perch and eventually burn itself out. But this fact did not come to light until after the next thunderstorm. Lightning hit a tree about a mile up the road toward town, and knocked a limb off. The limb fell on the power line. It broke.

At the time, Mr. Simpson's water works had been whirring merrily along in the Spring House, with belts slapping and the great flywheels revolving, and Lunt Moss groaning and moaning off in a corner. Several hours later, when the power came on again, all this activity had come to a halt. At the first surge of electricity, the motor huffed and puffed and fried and scorched, and dripped large amounts of tar onto the logs, but it couldn't start those flywheels moving by itself. Eventually the fuses came to the rescue, but there wasn't enough left inside that motor to make a good home telegraph set.

Mr. Simpson didn't say anything, but he came and he looked, and after a couple of days he returned with a new motor and a mechanical box that was labeled "Rheostat, Pat. Pending." Its purpose was to cut off the current as soon as there was a failure in the power source. It worked spendidly for about three years. Then it became apparent why the Pat. was Pending, because one time it didn't work and the new motor, confronted by the impossible task of starting up the flywheels, likewise sizzled itself to death. In the process, flaming tar dropped to the oil-impregnated logs, and it was too late to save the Spring House when the fireman arrived.

The red menace, still with a jagged hole in its cylinder, was a blackened mass of metal. The belts were gone. Half a dozen oil cans had added to the fuel. Only Lunt Moss survived. Subsequently powered by a Model T engine, it went on moaning its dirge, *Lunt . . . Moss, Lunt . . . Moss,* for a good many years to come.

chapter twelve

Sure, It's Westinghouse!

ELECTRICITY came to the farm in 1922. It arrived with wires, poles, transformers, and Jimmy Sinclair. Jimmy had contracted to install the wiring. Besides being energetic and knowledgeable about the new wonder, Jimmy whistled. He would arrive in the morning, he would whistle all day, and late in the afternoon he would depart, still whistling. After a week of this, my father began to refer to him as Whistler's Brother.

Wiring an old house at that time was no joke. The massive sills had to be bored by hand augers, and there was little rhyme or reason to the location of the upright timbers. Today these are called "studs" and are located sixteen inches on center, but in houses built prior to 1800, the uprights were placed about anywhere a carpenter felt like it. Some historians believe that rum influenced their judgment in the matter of uprights.

But Whistler's Brother was made of stern stuff. By constantly turning his augers and fishing wires, and constantly whistling, he installed wall fixtures throughout the house. He also got in a few outlets, though not nearly as many as he wanted; rather plain brass lights on the wall at eye level were the thing then. He did install an outlet below the dining-room table, which necessitated cutting a hole in the Oriental rug, but we all viewed it as the work of a true genius. He likewise installed a heavy-duty outlet for an electric stove in the kitchen.

He then proceeded to the barn and festooned the inside with wires, bulbs, and switches. From there, he whistled his way out to the chicken house, dragging his wires and boring his holes and nailing up fixtures until it seemed that every hen would have her own light.

He thoughtfully ran four wires to my father's workshop on the hill, so that my father could extinguish his kerosene lamp for the last time and convert to electric illumination with the rest of the farm.

By this time the power company had set its poles and strung its lines up the driveway. Near the house, it hung a giant transformer to one of these poles and connected the wires. Down in the cellar, a main switch that seemed large enough to handle the current for a small city was still open. Whistler's Brother was standing by, waiting to throw it in. Before he did, however, my father assembled the whole family about him and gave us a short talk on the Evolution of Mankind.

"Now, boys," he said, "when Jimmy throws that switch you will be seeing the end of one era and the beginning of a new one. Right now we are still in the era of the kerosene lamp. You've grown up with kerosene lamps. Every morning of your lives, your mother or Violet or somebody has collected all the lamps from all over the house, cleaned the globes, trimmed the wicks, and refilled them with kerosene. Tomorrow morning that chore will be gone forever. We are about to enter a new time-saving phase in the history of the world. During your lifetimes, you will see a dozen more inventions come into common use that will be just as important as this one. All right, Jimmy, throw it in."

Jimmy stopped whistling for an instant and seized the handle. Then he closed the switch with a solemnity usually reserved for bridge dedications. There was a flash of sparks when the switch closed, and instantly we were standing thunderstruck and awed in the new era. Every light in the house came on in a blazing glare of incandescent illumination. We kids scampered from room to room to make sure the new marvel worked everywhere. After that we ran to the barn to see how the cows and the chickens liked Thomas Edison's invention. They apparently were taking it in stride, although one startled rooster did attempt to crow.

We were a pretty triumphant group that night, turning lights on and off throughout the house, shouting and hurraying at each new discovery. Probably the most remarkable of these was the fact that it was now possible to go upstairs without carrying a lamp in the right hand. And when we turned off a light, there was no lingering odor of kerosene smoke. My father had been right. A new era had come to the farm.

The full effects of it, however, were not realized until a cheerful man from the power company came down the drive one morning with a bold idea. He cornered my parents in the kitchen and sold them on the astonishing theory that cooking could be done better on an electric stove than on a coal burner.

"Look," he said, pointing to the big old-fashioned kitchen range that made that room so cozy on a cold morning, "wouldn't it be nice not to have to bring in coal, or carry out ashes, or shake the grates? You'd just turn a switch, and there would be your dinner cooking. If you want a four-hundred-degree oven, you set the switch and there you have it. On hot days, when you're through cooking, you turn the switches off, and your kitchen is comfortably cool. No more slaving over a coal stove, eh, Mrs. Paine?"

My mother thought that would be a fine idea, although it was Violet who did most of the slaving. And as usual, my father was fascinated with anything that could be turned on and off, so he told the power-company manager to send over the largest stove he had.

He did. It arrived in a crate that could have furnished the timbers for a small house. But the men finally got it apart with wrecking bars and hammers. Then they moved out the coal stove and brought in the new one.

It was a magnificent stove for its day. It had four big heating coils on the top, and an oven that could accommodate a thirty-pound turkey and still have room for a small pony. It,

85

too, was covered top and bottom with endless miles of coiled wire.

For a whole week, Violet produced meals that were every bit as good as any she had cooked on the coal stove. No longer did she have to bring in the coal, shake the grate, or carry out the ashes . . . just as the man had said. Manifestly, this stove could do anything that a coal stove could, and everybody was very pleased.

At least until the night when we all were taken up to Jack Grant's Cafe for dinner. It seemed that a roast beef that had been put in the cavernous oven had failed to cook. It hadn't even warmed up. My mother called the power company to report this sorry state of affairs right away, and off we went to Jack Grant's.

The power-company official promised to have a repairman here in the morning. He didn't state *which* morning, and perhaps he didn't intend to. Six days later a repairman did show up in the morning. He diagnosed the trouble as a burned-out coil and went off with the remains. A couple of weeks passed pleasantly enough without any baking, until finally the repairman returned with a new coil. This one survived for almost two weeks. More calls. More repairmen.

We had better luck with the heating units on the top of the stove. Three of them worked for a month before burning out. The other proved its stamina by remaining operative for perhaps two months. In each case, the repairman turned up shaking his head in some embarrassment and went off with the burned-out part. A week or so later he would come back and install a new one.

After each of these skirmishes, there was a noticeable cooling in my family's love affair with electricity. Although we kids preferred eating out at Jack Grant's, we were aware that our love of this form of recreation was not shared wholeheartedly by our parents.

Finally there came the evening when nothing on the stove worked. Because of either broken switches or burned-out heating coils, every unit had quit for good. When the repairman failed to show up the next day as promised, my father went to his typewriter after returning from Jack Grant's and pounded out an editorial he entitled "Service." He sent it to the state's daily newspaper, which was always happy to get a new viewpoint.

In a forthright manner, the editorial pointed out that prompt, efficient, and satisfactory service was the key to the sales of modern electrical appliances. He wrote that the electric stove was indeed an improvement on the coal stove, but what good was it if the service offered by the sales agent was poor and shaky? He wound up his editorial by answering his own question. Without effective service, the electric stove was worse than nothing.

Finally, he wrote that unless better service could be obtained, he was considering throwing the piece of junk out the door and reinstating the reliable coal stove.

Now there followed a series of coincidences. A neighbor and friend, Jim Chamberlin, who had known the president of Westinghouse when they lived in Philadelphia, sent a clipping of the editorial to him. Perhaps this little squib would interest the president of a great electrical manufacturing company.

It certainly did. He called Jim Chamberlin on the phone and substantially what he said was this: "That's the best editorial on service that I have ever read. It says just what I have been trying to tell our dealers for months. They've got to give service. I wonder if you could get permission to have copies made and sent to all our dealers?"

Jim Chamberlin replied, "Why not call him yourself?"

Soon after that, my father got to talk to the president of Westinghouse Electric. What kind of stove had he been writing about? That was a good one. It was a Westinghouse! Sure, the president had his permission to reprint the editorial if he thought it might do some good.

There was a moment of silence at the other end of the phone while the president regained his composure. That the editorial had been written about one of his own stoves had not occurred to him. Then he asked what dealer had sold the stove. My father gave him the name of the power company.

What happened next became one of Mr. Storer's favorite stories, which he told proudly for years. Mr. Storer was the manager of the power company. He told me the story a hundred times, and, although the years passed, the tale never changed.

"There I was, just getting into bed when the phone rang," Storer would say. "Nellie the operator said there was a long-distance call from Philadelphia. So I said, 'All the way from Philadelphia?' and Nellie said, 'That's right. All the way from Philadelphia.' So I said, 'All right, Nellie, put him on.' There was some clicking on the wire, and then there I was talking to the president of Westinghouse Electric. Imagine it! And he said sort of brusque-like, 'Storer, did you sell a Ralph Paine of Durham one of our electric stoves?'

"I replied proudly that I had. It was something to have the president of a big company call up at night and congratulate me on it. We'd been handling the company's appliances for just a short time, and I didn't think anybody had noticed our effort.

"But then in the next sentence, the president said, 'Look, Storer, I don't care what you're doing now. And I don't care how you do it. Carry it over on your back, if you have to. But have a new stove at Paine's house by eight o'clock in the morning. Have you got that straight?' I said I had. I would call a couple of the boys and get them in early, and the stove would be there at eight o'clock in the morning, sure.

"Then he said good night and hung up. Right away, Nellie down at the telephone office called back and asked who had been calling all the way from Philadelphia, so I told her the truth. The president of Westinghouse Electric. A little personal matter. 'Yeah,' she said, 'I heard that part about the stove, but I couldn't figure out who it was you were talking to. My, think of it. The president of a big company talking right here through my switchboard.' I thanked her for her interest, and then asked her to get me Slim Davis on the phone, and after that Dick Plumby. 'They've got to get up early tomorrow morning.' "

At eight o'clock the stove was here on a truck, not on Mr. Storer's back as the president had suggested. It was a better model all around. Its heating units didn't burn out for a whole year, and when they did, they were replaced within the hour.

Here at the farm, the transition from kerosene and coal to electricity had been completed, thanks to Whistler's Brother and an editorial written at white heat.

chapter thirteen

Refrigeration

I still call an electric refrigerator an ice chest, even though it defrosts itself automatically, freezes sixty pounds of food, and produces ice cubes on an assembly-line basis.

That's because I grew up alongside an ice chest. For several summers, it was my assigned task to appease its insatiable appetite for ice. Besides, calling a refrigerator an ice chest seems quaint to some people. It's like saying "whoa" to a tractor.

Our ice chest was a four-door model manufactured by the White Mountain Company, and it was set into one of the kitchen walls. The top compartment was capable of storing fifty pounds of ice, which kept the other three compartments moderately cool for two days during the summer months. Sometimes, as the cake of ice got smaller and the day grew hotter, the temperature differential between the inside of the chest and the kitchen was barely noticeable. Then there would be a thunderstorm late in the afternoon, and the milk would turn sour.

This gave rise to an unshakable belief of my mother's that it was the electricity in the air that soured the milk. Her theory did not recognize the fact that thunderstorms generally occurred on very warm days when the ice chest was falling behind in its duties. Even though we youngsters knew everything at the age of fifteen and had installed a telegraph set between the house and the barn, thus demonstrating our Edison-like understanding of electricity, my mother went right on believing that thunderstorms somehow got into that White Mountain ice chest and curdled the milk.

She likewise believed that an open window during a storm drew the lightning into the house. This was on a par with her frequently expressed caution about drinking cold water on a hot day. A man on the neighboring farm had been haying and had gone to the spring to slake his thirst. When the others found him, he was lying beside the spring dead, the victim of a huge, round ice ball in his stomach. That made quite an impression on me at the time. I imagined this medical phenomenon as being about the size of a croquet ball.

There were several marked differences between maintaining an ice chest in those days and plugging a cord into an electric outlet. In the first place, the ice had to be cut from the mill pond in January. The best time was after a few snappy nights had frozen the water to a depth of eighteen inches and not much snow had fallen. But there had to be some snow; otherwise the two-horse pung would have been useless. This was the wholesale end of the business, and I never got into that much. Will Burrows and Arthur Terri cut the ice into blocks and brought them back behind Charley Horse and Old Dick. They performed this task for the Chamberlins, who lived about a mile nearer the village, and for us. The reasoning behind this was simple. We owned a two-horse pung but only one horse. Jim Chamberlin did not have a pung, but he owned Old Dick.

Some years earlier, Charley and Old Dick had founded their own mutual admiration society. Such was their adoration of each other that they seldom cared to be separated. The Chamberlins maintained better fences than the Paines, so as a consequence Charley felt an obligation to do most of the calling. When he was pastured out, he generally got the urge to pay his call at five o'clock in the morning.

He was not a dainty, light-footed horse; when he laid a

hoof down on the ground, he took it for granted that it would remain there until he decided to pick it up again. In other words, he clomped. So Jim Chamberlin would telephone my father a couple of hours later: "Ralph, that darn horse of yours came clomping down my driveway again at five-fifteen this morning. Woke up the whole family. Can't you keep him tied up?" My father would make a few neighborly remarks and send somebody off with a halter to fetch Charley home. Only a long-time friendship with my father, plus Charley's indispensable role in getting the ice for both families, prevented Mr. Chamberlin from calling in a glue manufacturer.

When the ice cutting was on, Charley Horse and Old Dick would come clomping down our driveway with a couple of tons of ice on the pung. Each chunk was clear as glass and identical to all the others. This was because the Chamberlins also owned a one-horse ice-maker: a set of metal teeth made fast to a wide plank, which was dragged across the ice to groove out the squares. Then Will and Arthur followed these lines with their saws.

Our own ice house was located about a hundred feet from the kitchen door and was well hidden by pine trees. Charley and Old Dick clomped a sort of road into it over a period of years, and now they would come to a stop in front of the door, steaming in the cold air. Will and Arthur would pick up their tongs and start the chunks down a long chute to the bottom of the ice house. These were then placed about four inches apart with at least a two-foot space around the sides of the whole stack. Then they had to fill around and between and over the ice chunks with sawdust. This made the best insulation then available. It also gave the ice house a woodsy, damp aroma that was pleasing, particularly on a hot summer day.

The wholesale end of the business was usually accomplished in a week. By that time, the tiers of ice had been built up to within a few feet of the roof. A couple of tons of sawdust were then shoveled carefully over the top, and Will and Arthur would depart to get in a year's supply of ice for the Chamberlins.

No one went near the ice house until May; we counted on our New England winters to keep our food cool, and they seldom failed us. Every farmhouse had its vegetable cellar and its "cold room," and of course its woodshed. Our milk seldom soured during these months, and that proved to my mother that it was the lightning that curdled it in the summer — we didn't have much lightning during the cold months.

Along about May fifteenth, however, the weather would turn warm and the butter would get soft, and I would be sent off to the ice house with a wheelbarrow, a pair of tongs, and a shovel. An ice pick would be stuck in a two-by-four beside the door where it had been left the previous September. Uncovering the ice was always fun. Although I knew everything about almost anything, thermal dynamics was not one of my long suits. I was always astonished to hear the shovel make contact with a solid piece of ice. Even more incredible was the fact that the chunks of ice had not shrunk perceptibly.

I doubt if a fourteen-year-old boy today would know how to cut a block of ice into two equal pieces. He'd understand how to turn a knob inside a refrigerator to make it colder, all right, but he would just make a mess of things with an ice pick. He'd end up with a lot of slivers.

Will Burrows had taught me the trick. A gentle, persistent picking in a straight line across the top of a chunk was better than walloping it hard a few times, which only produced small pieces that got lost in the sawdust. Under Will's tutelage I became an expert. I could split a chunk of ice almost as evenly as though I had halved it with a saw. In the light of recent progress, this wasn't much of an accomplishment, and it certainly had its limitations as far as a career was concerned, but it came in handy at the time.

Having split a chunk in this fashion, I would grip it with the tongs and lift it into the wheelbarrow. Then I would push the vehicle to the kitchen door and wash off the sawdust with a hose.

Now I never saw fit to write to the White Mountain Company to ask why they put the ice compartment at the *top* of their chest, but it always seemed to me that they could have used one of the lower spaces without noticeably changing the temperature of the other three. As it was, their designer came up with an ice compartment that was level with my eye, and raising a fifty-pound chunk that high with hands turning numb from the cold was quite a trick. Often it slipped out of my grasp before I could push it onto the tray. This caused a bit of commotion, particularly if the cat was hanging around looking for a handout. Once a chunk landed on its long yellow tail, and three weeks later a third of that tail dropped off in the living room. The cat should have found a lesson there, but it didn't. The following summer another ice cake subtracted another couple of inches from that tail.

This complicated method of keeping food cold came to an end the winter that Freddie Jenkins Senior decided Jim Chamberlin had said something to him that he didn't care for. Freddie Senior was like that. Touchy. If he didn't like the way you spoke to him in the morning, he might work up a feud that was good for a year. He had one feud going that dated back a couple of decades before the Civil War, passed on from one generation to the next, like the family Bible.

This feud with Jim Chamberlin was only a little one. It was good for no more than a couple of years, but it commenced one winter just before ice-cutting time. As it happened, Freddie owned the old cider mill at the end of the mill pond. He was also under the impression that he owned the pond itself.

Will Burrows and Arthur Terri were filing their ice saws and overhauling the pung, and feeding Charley Horse and Old Dick on oats in preparation for the annual ice frolics. Both ice houses had been cleaned out and fresh sawdust hauled in. Then, the night before the cutting out was scheduled to begin, Freddie played his trump card. He opened the sluice gates under his cider press and drained the mill pond dry. Will and Arthur discovered this the next morning when they arrived at their chosen spot for bringing in the ice. The ice was there all right, but it was lying on the bottom of the pond, and the slope to the bank was better than forty-five degrees. No horses could have negotiated it, least of all Charley and Old Dick with a pung behind them.

So everybody sat around for a couple of days, cussing and threatening and talking with lawyers, and trying to figure out what to do next. The talk about it was interspersed with some merriment among the old-timers along Main Street. The Chamberlins and the Paines were relatively recent arrivals in town, and a few felt that Freddie "had sure pulled a good

95

one" on the newcomers.

In a way, that feud was a good thing. It hastened the decision by both families to venture into electric refrigeration, which, this time, appeared to be here to stay. Ours arrived with the cooling coils on the top and a thermostat and a way to make it colder or warmer by turning a knob. It was little short of a miracle. The pung was brought back and left beside the woodpile. Its four heavy iron runners are still there, though all the wood has rotted away. The ice house stayed up until the 1939 hurricane, and the ice tongs are still hanging in the garage.

One other significant change in our lives was brought about by the new invention. For some reason, lightning couldn't get into this modern ice chest and sour the milk.

chapter fourteen

The Durham Pageant

DURING the 1920s most of the towns along the New Hampshire seaboard celebrated three hundred years of existence. There was a logical reason for this: the first colonists had sailed into Portsmouth about three centuries before and the very strong current of the Piscataqua River just swept them on upstream to what are now Durham, Dover, Newington, Newmarket, and Exeter.

Along about 1923, certain people in Durham decided that it would be a fine thing if the town put on a pageant to mark the three-hundredth anniversary of its founding. These were most likely the ladies of the women's club, who were big on this type of activity. The historical records were a little sketchy as to the exact time of year that our first settlers stepped on Durham soil, but the consensus was that nobody in his right mind would have been foolhardy enough to step outside the cozy taverns of Portsmouth during the winter months. Therefore the settlers must have come in the summer. Furthermore, they probably got here during the second week of August, because that was the most convenient time to stage the pageant.

My father, being the only full-time author in the village, was recruited to write the scenario. This looked to be easy enough at first; there never was much dialogue in a pageant. The usual procedure was for a bunch of Indians to shoot arrows across the river at the white settlement, and then the settlers would come storming out of the woods with their muzzleloaders and shoot the daylights out of the Indians. This would restore peace and order, and the colonists could go on about their business.

The Durham pageant was complicated somewhat by the fact that a certain faction of men and boys wanted to come rowing or sailing up the river and beat the tar out of the Indians. Whether there was any historical basis for this was uncertain, but if you're going to have a pageant along a river bank, you may as well bring in some boats. So far, the script was coming along about as expected. There would be a lot of arrows flying around in the air, and a surprising number of muzzleloaders in usable condition had been unearthed in barns and woodsheds. They could be counted upon to make a bit of noise.

But after a few weeks, it turned out that almost everybody in town was a pageant director. Little episodes began to be added. Mel Perkins, the blacksmith, wanted to dash into the settlement on horseback as Paul Revere, shouting the alarm that the British were at Portsmouth. Nobody knew for sure whether Paul ever did get to Portsmouth, but if he did, he came one hundred and fifty years after the Indian fight that was supposed to be taking place on the opposite bank. My father, figuring that Mel would dash in on horseback anyway, changed the script to fit the dash. The pageant would embrace the first one hundred and fifty years of the town's existence.

With this alteration, even more boats could be used on the river. In fact, there could be a second flotilla, returning from Portsmouth after having looted Fort William and Mary of its gunpowder. This was a proud incident in the history of Durham, and little children were teethed on it. According to local legend, a bunch of men led by the indomitable General John Sullivan floated downriver to New Castle, scared a couple of British guards half to death, and returned on the tide as far as Portsmouth, where they spent a couple of days and nights examining the local taverns. In fact, local history indicates they dallied so long in that lively city that the river froze over before they got back, and they had to chop their way through the ice for the last mile or two. Apparently they were able to do this with a pleasant cheerfulness, being full of good short lobsters and rum.

In a sort of indirect way, their brave deed won the Battle of Bunker Hill, when the stolen gunpowder was used to good effect against its former owners. This in turn showed the British that they had not started any picnic, and from there it was but a short step to the Battle of Yorktown. So the fact that the Americans won the Revolution could be traced back to that gang of Durham men who had swiped the gunpowder from the New Castle fort and then lived it up for a while in Portsmouth.

Some of this was more or less true, and as far as the pageant was concerned, it provided us with something to do after the Indians had been slaughtered in the first act.

As the days passed, numerous other things got added. Somebody felt there should be an old-fashioned outdoor school, so there was. I was to play one of the naughty school-children and go fishing on the bank of the river. Then Elmer Rand, playing the truant officer, would grab me by the scruff of the neck and lead me back to my desk, where presumably I would go on with my labors. This was a humorous touch, to keep the crowd in stitches while the second flotilla came rowing up the stream with the stolen gunpowder.

As the scenario progressed, the committee decided that the best way to end the pageant was to have Sam Craig, playing a town father, approach a now subdued and friendly Indian chief and smoke a peace pipe on the stone embankment just below the bridge. In the background, men and women would be singing a hymn as they stepped out the door of the church. This seemed like a fitting close to a long afternoon of exploding gunpowder and howling Indians. The hymn had been selected and practiced by the would-be congregation. It was a good hymn, and it said just the right things, but some purist pointed out that it hadn't been written until 1870. The committee immediately went into a tailspin. Quite a few accusations and counteraccusations were bruited about, but peace was restored by the selection of a hymn written about 1820. That made it slightly more credible anyway. The words weren't as lively, but the tune was catchy.

Nowadays, it is doubtful if more than ten people in town would willingly dress themselves in Indian breechcloths and decorate their faces to celebrate the founding of the country, much less a little New Hampshire village. It was different then. Grown men enthusiastically daubed their faces and bodies with a copper-colored theatrical paint and twanged their bows and practiced war whooping.

On the settlers' side, women sewed and stitched to make costumes for their warriors. These were patterned after the standard Miles Standish model shown in every history textbook: tall hat, big buckles, knee pants — and, for some extraordinary reason, one coat of mail, which was assigned to Sam Craig. Sam was to play the big final scene on the river bank with the Indian chief. There was some significance to this. Sam Craig had fought Indians at the Battle of Wounded Knee, so he could be trusted to deal with Will Chesley, who was to play the chief, in a smart fashion. For some years, there had been slight traces of animosity between these two men, owing, I believe, to a matter of insincerity in the sale of a horse. Eventually, this was to provide a spectacular and unrehearsed climax to the village pageant.

Well, on the day of the pageant, the weather was perfect. It was one of those August days that New England produces every four or five years: no clouds, soft sunshine, and a mild breeze. Mrs. Buzzel called it a weather-breeder, but predicted that things would remain in fine shape until the end of the pageant. Meanwhile, the incredible beauty of the day brought out the crowd by the hundreds. People came with picnics and seated themselves on the hill above the river bank, and chatted and waited for the great drama to unfold.

Amazingly, the pageant got underway almost on time. The tide was the reason for this: the two marine sequences had to take place before the implacable pull of the moon emptied the river and left General Sullivan and the Indians standing knee deep in saltwater mudflats.

At two o'clock all the players were in their places. The Indians crouched hot and sweaty in their wigwams on the north side of the river. The settlers, on the south side, were going about their business. School was in session, and my fish pole had been hidden down by the bank in preparation for the comedy act with the truant officer. Behind the church, which in fact had been the town jail for a hundred or so years, Will Burrows was fooling around with his muzzleloader. He had dropped in a sizable amount of powder, primed the pan, and was adjusting the flint when it unexpectedly went off with a great whoosh. The sound of the explosion carried across the river to the perspiring Indians, and the war was on.

The Indians burst from the tents and let fly their arrows, the points of which had been padded just in case they came down on some unlucky settler's neck. School was disbanded, and we went and hid behind the jail until the next act. The womenfolk, who had been doing their washing and gossiping along the river bank, fled for cover while the brave settlers emerged from the brush, firing their muzzleloaders.

It was all pretty realistic. The smell of black powder was strong, and smoke hung over the beleaguered settlement. As this was taking place, more Indians made their way upriver in their canoes. The script now called for a renewal of the shooting and the killing of six or seven Indians. The others were to flee downriver, change costumes, and then come back with the Sullivan party.

Skooch Langley brought on the first crisis. He was scheduled to get shot by the settlers and flop down on the bottom of his canoe. But when it came his turn to bite the dust, he didn't flop down. No, indeed. He flopped over the side with his head underwater. When it remained there for several minutes, his mother went screaming through the settlers' army and into the water. Its depth at this tide was about four feet, so she started to swim. As she neared the canoe, she called out, "Skooch — Skooch — where did they hit you?" Then she got hold of his hair and yanked his head out of the water. Whereupon, Skooch gave his mother a look of disgust and wailed, "Now you've spoiled everything, Ma. I've got a piece of hose that I breathe through. It was to make it look more real. But now you've spoiled it."

Mrs. Langley, still suffering from fright and cold water, swam back to shore and departed for home.

By this time settlers had routed the redskins, and were returning to their placid life on the river bank. Ladies turned spinning wheels, others washed clothes that had already been washed several times, men pretended to till the fields, and school kept. I was about ready to stage my bit of drollery when a lone horseman was observed pounding across the bridge just above the Indian camp. It was Mel Perkins, all right, and almost immediately a sense of dread fell over the pageant. For he wheeled into the Indian camp, pulled his steed back on its haunches, and bellowed: "One ish by shee. Two ish by land. Shee Bristish is coming."

An Indian stuck his head out of a teepee and said in a whisper that carried well into the middle of the village, "For gosh sake, Mel. You're drunk. You're on the wrong side of the river."

"Who shez sho?" yelled Mel, running a hand across his eyes in hopes that it might improve his vision.

By now, the Indian realized that the situation was not going to be improved by pointing out the difference in culture, skin color, language, or origins between Native Americans and immigrant Anglo Saxons. So he took direct action. "Get the heck out of here, Mel," he said, and belted the horse a stinging swipe on the rear with his bow.

Drunk or sober, Mel could stick to a horse, and as his reared and bolted for the blacksmith shop up in the village, he trailed a string of curses that added heat to an already warm day.

His going left an awful stillness along the upper reaches of the Oyster River. Spinning wheels stopped; men ceased tilling; women hung motionless over their washtubs. The spectators sat transfixed, as though they had suddenly been turned to stone. But as the clattering hoofbeats receded in the distance on Church Hill, everybody let out his breath at the same time, and laughter rolled down from the slope. They were getting their money's worth that day.

Obviously there was some ad libbing to be done, and one of the settlers did it. Through a megaphone he announced the news that Mel was supposed to have brought: British soldiers were on their way to reinforce the fort at New Castle. General Sullivan and a group of heroes had seized the powder and would be coming up the river directly. And sure enough, as he finished speaking, the flotilla of boats swept around the point. They landed without incident, and the powder kegs were brought ashore and placed in a wagon. This was driven off and Act III was almost over.

Except that Sam Craig and Will Chesley still had to meet on the opposite shore and smoke the peace pipe. When the time came, Sam clanked down to a boat in his coat of mail and was rowed to the other side. The chief emerged from his teepee and went to the water's edge with his pipe. As Sam raised himself and his weighty garment from the boat, Will reached out to take his hand.

No one knows truly what happened. Perhaps Will Chesley was thinking back to the horse he had bought from Sam a few years before. Perhaps not. Anyway, their handclasp failed to materialize. Sam's ponderous coat of mail threw him off balance. The boat rocked, and Sam toppled into the water. In an instant he shot from view, dragged down by his metal costume. For several seconds, Will and the settler who had rowed Sam across the river stared down into the murky water with disbelief. They knew that Sam was a strong swimmer, but the odds had been changed by the suit he was wearing. Dropping his peace pipe, Will plunged into the water.

The next instant, Will and Sam appeared at the surface, the latter sputtering recriminations that would have done credit to Mel Perkins. Then they found their footing and slowly sloshed out of the river together. They were troupers to the last. With water still streaming from his costume, Sam strode over to the spot where the peace pipe lay and thrust it into his mouth. He passed it to the somewhat bedraggled Indian chief, who pretended to suck on it. Finally, they shook hands, as the script said they should, and Durham was safe at last. Across the river, the congregation was engrossed in the 1820 hymn.

I could tell you what Sam said to Will when they were emerging from the water together, but I won't. However, I can disclose that if Will had been a real Indian chief, the war would have gone on for another twenty-five years, at least.

chapter fifteen

Farm and Home Week

NEW Hampshire has had numerous governors during its history. Some of these have been good, some indifferent, and at least one should have been sent to the reform school when he was young.

My only truck with any of these chief executives occurred one summer when I caused Governor Bass to move faster than any other New Hampshire official before or since. In fact, I would say that Governor Bass was the fastest-moving politician in the whole history of America. Somewhere in the files of Pathé News, there must still reside about thirty feet of aging film showing how he won this title. But even if the celluloid has deteriorated with time and can no longer be run, I know all the facts connected with this record event because I helped him accomplish it.

This singular affair took place during a Farm and Home Week at the state college. In those days, the Extension Service sponsored six days of riotous living for the country folk every August. It was usually scheduled just ahead of the Durham Day Picnic so that everybody could go home at the end smelling of cows, horses, sheep, hogs, clams, and lobsters.

The best way to describe Farm and Home Week is to call it a country fair without the trotters or the midway. It featured livestock and vegetable displays, prizes, some good clean talks in the evening, and a parade. This last was important enough to attract the governor down from Concord to shake a few hands and, he hoped, garner some votes.

Most of us boys who lived outside the village took the affair pretty seriously. We would enter our best squash and beans and beets and carrots in the contests. Or if we discovered a potato that resembled a human face, we would put that on display. There were also contests for the best apple jelly and the best jar of beans — for the girls — but these weren't very interesting to anybody except their mothers.

The parade was the big thing, really. There were ribbons for the prettiest float and the most original float, and for the most *meaningful* float. The year I won the blue ribbon for the most original float was also the year Governor Bass established his claim to immortality. We did it together, in fact.

Prior to this final triumph, I had driven the pony in a couple of Farm and Home Week parades. We attracted a lot of notice but failed to bring home any ribbons. To correct this situation, I abandoned the pony motif one spring and set about training two Ayrshire calves as oxen. There was nothing on a farm so lacking in IQ as a calf, unless it was a hen, but these two young heifers were hand weaned and entirely docile. They were unable to understand verbal commands, but they responded nicely to a stick from behind or a rap on the nose. And while their sense of direction was hopeless, they could be pushed along if everything else failed.

After two or three months of pushing and hauling and shouting, I had a bona fide pair of female oxen. They would plod along with the pony cart just like a two-horse team. But pulling a simple cart was not likely to win any ribbons at Farm and Home Week.

No, the thing to do was to go after a prize for the most original float. I wasn't likely to come up with the most *meaningful* display, because that meant getting in some propaganda for the Extension Service. And the ribbon for the prettiest float always went to some fool girls' club that got the mothers to sit up half the night weaving flowers into patterns.

So I took aim at the originality prize. The body of the pony cart had to come off. When this was done, I built a miniature hayrack. Some old-timers called it a hayrick, but "hayrack" was the way I learned it. Anyway, it was mine, and it was a hayrack. I nailed boards to the cross braces as a platform for the hay. Then I bored holes about a foot apart along all four edges, to hold the upright stakes that would keep the hay from falling off. The construction was copied exactly from a larger model behind the barn.

Into the holes, I stuck dowels — round, machine-shaped pieces of wood that could be bought in four-foot lengths and were indispensable at the time to any twelve-year-old boy. They came in various sizes from a quarter-inch to a full inch. I bought the half-inch dowels for the hayrack.

Around the top of the full-grown hayrack behind the barn, a two-by-four held the uprights in place. Holes had been bored in it to correspond with the holes in the platform, and the whole thing looked like a crib. My intention was to use a one-by-two board to top off the dowels on my hayrack. However, the dowels stuck up so straight and sturdy that it didn't seem necessary to put on the top rail. They would be covered anyway.

Then I pitched on the hay from the loft in the barn and shaped the load. This was something that every farm kid knew how to do, and I had done it on the big hayrack a couple dozen times that summer. When this task was completed, I hitched up the calves and took them for a practice spin around the barnyard. They made quite a sight. Except for minor discrepancies, the whole rig looked like a miniature duplicate of haying time fifty years earlier.

This, then, was my entry. On parade day, I pushed and hauled my calves the two miles to town. They seemed to enjoy it and took in the sights as they ambled along. They even behaved pretty well during the parade; only once did they get up on the sidewalk. We went around the sports field of the college and ended up at the far corner in front of Governor Bass, who was viewing the affair from the bleachers.

Pathé News had a camera grinding away at the various floats, and when it came my turn to perform, the cameraman had an inspiration.

"Hey, Governor," he called up to the stands. "How about coming down and posing with this kid and his hayrack?"

The governor was delighted. He had probably been looking on with envy at all the publicity that was going elsewhere. So he asked my name and how long it was going to be before I could vote. I gave him straightforward answers. Then the cameraman said: "Hey, sonny, do you think you could give the governor a ride on your wagon?"

Governor Bass replied for me. "Sure you could, couldn't you, boy?" He was well aware that Pathé News was shown in dozens of motion-picture houses throughout the state. The film would depict a busy governor, but one never so busy that he didn't have time for the farm folk and their problems.

So the camera started whirring, and the governor vaulted from the hitch pole onto the load of hay. In the next instant he became the fastest-moving politician in the history of New Hampshire. For he came back up again — several feet into the air. Exactly how many was never officially determined. Some say it was ten feet; others contended that the distance couldn't have been more than six. But it wasn't the distance that mattered. It was the speed. There were so few things with which to compare it. The speed of sound? The speed of lightning? He was in that category.

At the same moment, he let out a bawl that startled the calves into motion. That was fortunate, because when he came down, my hayrack moved forward. This time he stayed put. The uncapped dowel on which he had first impaled himself had lost the range. The cameraman, meanwhile, not knowing about dowels, was enthralled by our active governor. What had started out as a routine new picture had unexpectedly turned into a gymnastic exhibition.

But politicians were politicians even then. As we went by the camera, the governor grinned bravely and waved one hand at it. The other hand was busily exploring his sit-down area. As soon as we had passed the cameras, I smacked the calves a couple of times on the nose and they stopped. The governor got down from the hayrack gingerly and patted me on the shoulder.

"That was a fine ride, boy, but you ought to put a rail on

top of your stakes." He was one of our smarter governors.

The next week, Pathé News did devote a few minutes to Farm and Home Week at the college, and I saw it twice. My calves looked great, and the hayrack was cute, but the outstanding part was Governor Bass of New Hampshire establishing the world record for vertical speed.

chapter sixteen

Dashing Through the Snow

REGARDLESS of what others may remember about sleighing fifty years ago, I am going to stick to the truth. Mostly it was cold, miserable work. The basic problem was that the horse or pony got the exercise and kept warm, while the passengers were forced to sit still in the open air for a considerable period of time. Furthermore, the sleigh was poorly conceived and designed. No attempt was made to enclose the passenger area the way the manufacturers of buggies did. The vehicle that was intended for use during the coldest months of the year was constructed in such a way that it offered about as much protection from the elements as a pine plank.

The curved dashboard, which was usually rather ornate, served principally as a bulwark against the bombardment of snowballs that flew from the horse's hind hooves. Otherwise, the one-horse open sleigh was just that. Open.

Over a span of fifty years, my memory of sleighing has not mellowed one whit. First of all there was the problem of putting a bridle on the pony. This meant warming the bit in the bare hands, for, without this protocol, the cold metal would have peeled the skin from the animal's tongue. This was followed by an ill-natured tussle between a couple of rows of great, yellow teeth before the pony agreed to let me put on his bridle.

If he had been standing in his stall for two or three days, he came out of it in a fashion that could only be described as spirited, and getting him hitched between the shafts was generally a rough-and-tumble affair that involved a good deal of loud conversation. Assuming that both participants survived this battle, the sleigh ride was almost ready to begin. But first the soapstones that were heating in the oven had to be placed on the floor of the sleigh. They didn't retain their heat for long, and they melted rubber boots, but they were better than nothing. On a trip to town, for example, the soapstones kept the driver's feet warm at least as far as the first watering trough, just past Lawrence Page's house and about fifty yards from the end of our driveway.

I have never known what a live buffalo smells like, but I can remember precisely the aroma that exuded from a pelt after it had been detached from its owner and made into a robe for sleigh riders. It had vigor and strength and pungency. Once it had become wet — say from falling snow — a sleigher was hard put to decide whether to die of the cold or of suffocation. In its damp state, a buffalo robe had all the sweetness and charm of a skunk hit by an automobile.

Obviously, there must have been a few winter days during those years when sleighing was a happy adventure. However, they don't stand out. I recall most attempts as endless tests of endurance accompanied by zero-degree temperatures and a stiff wind that always blew directly opposite to the direction in which I was going.

One trick was to get out and run alongside the sleigh to keep from freezing. The exercise got the pulse moving again, at least into the low forties, and the temperature of the body rose into the high eighties. Both hands, however, remained numb and often ached for hours after one of these outings. It was standard procedure to run them under a cold-water tap for a few minutes to draw out the frost. Never hot water — my mother was as opposed to hot water in the winter as she was to iced drinks in the summer.

On the other hand, the pony always arrived home steaming in the cold air and anxious to get back to eating. But he had to be rubbed down with a grain bag first so he wouldn't catch cold. This was a rule that had been drummed into me from the first day the animal arrived. Whether there was any validity to it I never knew. Rubbed down or not, he always managed to get through the night, even when the drying process involved only a token pass down his back with the grain bag.

There was, however, one sleigh ride each year that I did enjoy. That was after the first snow, when the pony had to be driven up to Mel Perkins's blacksmith shop for shoeing. This establishment was the headquarters for four or five men who had somehow learned to live without working. They enjoyed their leisure at the blacksmith shop, keeping regular hours and sitting around on benches or piles of horseshoes from eight o'clock in the morning until noon. They would knock off for an hour or two and return to their homes for lunch, and, unless they got trapped by their wives, they would be back in full force at two o'clock. From then until five they talked, made comments on Mel's workmanship, and occasionally turned the handle on the forge for him. But forging was strictly extracurricular; the main course of study encompassed men, women, horses, and cider. A kid could learn a lot in a classroom like that.

Mel himself was industrious and competent when shoeing a horse or a pony. He could calm down the most fractious beast in a matter of seconds. Perhaps he talked horse. If so, he mixed it in with a lot of basic, unprintable English. But it was a fact that an animal that was kicking and snorting and pounding the floor to splinters at one instant would be docile the next, after Mel had said something to it in their secret language.

The smell of a blacksmith shop was also pretty intriguing. It combined soft coal smoke, seared hooves, sweaty horses, men who only bathed on Saturday nights, and cider. Altogether it was a charming atmosphere.

Mel and his students always liked to see me bring the pony in. The little stallion afforded the class an hour or two of ribald comparative anatomy, with comments ranging from the jocular to the downright envious. While this was going on, Mel expertly fitted the pony with new shoes and then screwed in the caulks — sharp pieces of iron that could be replaced if they were worn out during the winter. A horse or pony without caulks on his shoes was forever falling down as soon as the roads became slick. A human being slipping on ice or snow is a pretty ludicrous sight, but a horse that loses his footing is a catastrophe; he appears to have eighteen legs, all of them in motion. Furthermore, a horse isn't designed to get up. It is miraculous that he can do it at all.

But once Mel had put on the winter shoes, the pony was as sure-footed on ice as he was on bare earth. It was easy to see why. When he stepped on my foot, which he did as often as he could, I knew it. The caulks bit in like chisels.

After I paid Mel two dollars for the job, I generally stayed around for a while continuing my education. It was my judgment then, and it has never changed, that the conversation that flowed around Mel's forge was more witty, more erudite, and more worthwhile than any talk that five or six college professors could generate sitting around a seminar table. Primarily, the blacksmith-shop dwellers were sociologists. They studied the mores of each other, the college people, the town, and that part of the United States of America situated north of the Massachusetts line and bounded on the other sides by the Atlantic Ocean, Vermont, Maine, and Canada.

Mel had only one rule at his shop. If a woman brought in a horse to be shod, she was treated like a lady. Profanity died, the quips became less sharp, and Mel's dialogues with the horse became masterpieces of understatement. No woman was ever embarrassed at that blacksmith shop.

But it was a strain on all of them. One day I arrived just as the wife of a faculty member was driving off with her newly shod horse. Inside the shop, a bottle was being passed from hand to hand, and one of the regulars was mincing around, remarking in what he thought was an English accent: "A little more sugar in your tea, Duchess?"

chapter seventeen

The Grammar School

COMPARED to the magnificent brick structures that now house the Oyster River Cooperative School System, the old Durham Grammar School was a primitive affair. It contained eight rooms, a center staircase, separate facilities for boys and girls (called "the basement," though they weren't in the basement), and a manual training shop that *was* in the basement.

Outside, the school playground consisted of a half-acre of mud and rocks on which were installed a revolving swing and a teeter board. In the spring, enough worn-out bases to form a crude baseball diamond were borrowed or stolen from the college; in the fall, the older and more adept manual-training scholars made and erected two goal posts. Except among the most highly educated, these were pronounced "gool posts." We also kicked gools.

The physical-education program was so primitive that we had no coaches, no cheerleaders, no band, no official athletic teams, and of course no gymnasium. But we did boast a first-rate bunch of marble players who operated on the south side of the school building, in the spring, and in the mud.

A few feet from the back side of the school there was a board fence. I have since heard it said that the finest part of an education is to be obtained behind the school fence, but I never had much luck in this department, because the drop-off behind this one was so precipitous that it was hard to learn much there during recess. However, there was a pipe fence on the lower side of the playground that had a unique offering of its own. This had nothing to do with the school, but instead encompassed the town cemetery. Ordinarily, there is nothing of interest to young people in a cemetery, but this one was unusual. In addition to the gravestones and the pipe fence, it had a skeleton of sorts. Dogs had burrowed into a sunken grave and were gradually dismembering some earlier citizen of the town.

In fact, they spread him around over a considerable area before our anatomy lesson was concluded by town officials. I think a teacher squealed on us. Perhaps her curiosity had been aroused by our quiet fascination with local history after school hours. Anyway, the bones were there one afternoon, and the next day they had disappeared. There was fresh earth in the hole and the marker had been set up straight again. But I can testify that as a spur to learning there is nothing so effective as a human thigh bone. A very large percentage of that early anatomy class became doctors.

The school bus had not yet been invented in 1920, so we walked to school, a custom that perhaps accounted for the fact that we had no elaborate physical-education program. Moreover, most of us had chores to do when we got home. A kid who was expected to extract ten quarts of milk from a couple of cows every morning and night and clean out behind them and pitch down the hay didn't need to do gymnastics at school. He developed his muscles on the starboard side of a cow and in the hayloft and on the path to the schoolhouse.

That was a nice path. It was close to a mile long and wound over half a dozen stone walls and through a marsh. Toward the town end, it passed within a few feet of the Sullivan cemetery and the grave of General John Sullivan of Durham Pageant fame. We were reading about General Sullivan in American-history class and, by golly, we could stop off on the way home in the afternoon and slap his gravestone. Not too many American-history scholars could do that. Just us, and Lawrence Page and Tater Watson, and a couple of others who cut cross-lots from the Durham Point Road. This didn't compare to loose bones in the town cemetery, but it made history more interesting for a while.

The path to school then led down past the general's former home and across the mill pond bridge. Just to the left of the bridge stood a house in which lived a woman of some significance to us. About every two weeks or so, Mrs. Jenkins would come out her door waving her arms, and threaten us with, "You touch my Freddie again, and I'll have you put in the reform school. Yes, I mean you two Paine boys."

I don't think she could have made good on her threat because all we ever did to Freddie Junior was to hit him occasionally. But the threat had a scary ring to it. For some reason, "reform school" was bandied about a good deal by a lot of people during that era. It was the ultimate weapon of teachers, truant officers, school-board members, and Mrs. Jenkins; and it was impressive enough to send us running past Freddie's house at full speed until we had safely crossed the bridge. Once beyond that, we were free of the reform school for another few weeks.

But that ended the path, and we finished the rest of the walk to school on roads.

Now I am not going to contend that we received a better education in that dusty old building than the youngsters do in today's brick palaces. However, I think it was just as good, and a darn sight less expensive. The concept of the Whole Child had not yet caught on in Durham; we were thrown back to our parents every afternoon at three-thirty, and they were stuck with us until the following morning. This ancient philosophy had its advantages: it gave us time to study, and the teachers had an opportunity to prepare their work for the next day. The closest thing to the Oyster River Educational Workshop was the annual visit of the school-board members, who turned up unannounced one morning and sat at the back of each classroom for five or ten minutes. It must have been a dull task for them, listening to us go through the multiplication tables.

I don't believe that any of my teachers had ever taken a course in Education. These are the courses that teach students how to teach and that make up a high percentage of all the classes offered in the liberal-arts colleges of state universities.

So, being unaware of anything better, our teachers just taught. They didn't fool around much with our personalities or our social development. And if we showed signs of a learning disability, they sent us to the school nurse on Friday to have our eyes tested.

Occasionally, Ruth Seaver, the principal, would invite a person of some renown to come to our simple and rude building and talk to us. Admiral Sims was one of these, recently back from commanding the U.S. naval forces in Europe during World War I. He made quite a hit with his tales of naval action against the Hun, and our principal made an even bigger hit with him. "Ruth Seaver!" he exclaimed to my father that night at dinner. "What a peach!" Then, turning to me, he said, "Young man, how would you like to take me to school with you tomorrow?" He winked at me. "My arithmetic is getting a little rusty." The prospect of tugging Admiral Sims off to school was pretty exciting, but next morning he admitted he had to get back to helping the navy. Several decades passed before I came across a picture of our principal and realized that she had been not only an extremely efficient school principal, but also a pretty one. Perhaps that, and not the arithmetic, was what had caught the admiral's interest.

After a while, Ruth Seaver resigned her job and went off to get married. She had been in the Durham school only a few years, and during that time, no more than two hundred pupils had come under her tutelage. But in spite of the fact that the building had been archaic and our extracurricular activities nil, at least half of her pupils went to college — nine of them to Yale. Several earned advanced degrees in the sciences, and half a dozen others followed up their first anatomy course in the town cemetery and became doctors. One ragamuffin who heard Admiral Sims that day went off to the naval academy and became an admiral himself; when Dick O'Kane returned from World War II, President Truman hung the Congressional Medal of Honor around his neck.

All of this, of course, doesn't prove a thing, except that a kid learns just as well in a wooden building as he does in a magnificent display of brick and glass.

chapter eighteen
The Poultry Magnate

I don't know whether people go around saying about me that "he still has the first dollar he ever earned." If they do it doesn't bother me much because, as a matter of fact, I still have the first *fifty* dollars I ever earned. The money has been on deposit in the Strafford Savings Bank since 1923. I hope the folks there at the bank haven't done anything careless with it in the meantime.

Because it was money earned by selling eggs to Sam Runlett's store at fifteen cents a dozen. The producers of this valuable commodity were a flock of Rhode Island Reds that scrabbled out a living at the south end of the barn. They possessed a coop, and a yard that wasn't fenced very well, and they had some box nests.

Before the profit motive was brought into my hen keeping, the flock pretty much went its own way, reproducing its kind and a little besides for the breakfast table. The roosters usually ended up alongside dumplings on Sundays.

But by the time I turned fourteen, money had begun to have its uses. The Franklin movie theater had moved to town and was showing some exciting silent films that needed to be viewed. There were also peanuts and popcorn to be reckoned with.

That was when Sam Runlett and I entered into trade. In addition to being the postmaster, he also owned the local food store. The fact that my father was one of his best purchasers of groceries may have had something to do with Sam's enthusiasm for Paine eggs; he agreed to take all the eggs my flock could lay. Suddenly I was rich. I was Carnegie and Rockefeller put together. I was Durham Point's financial genius.

As a point of fact, I was. I've never had it so good. The market was assured and the product cost me nothing. Any expenses connected with the enterprise were borne by my father, so all I had to do was feed and water the hens, collect the eggs, and take the eggs to the store twice a week in the pony cart.

Here Sam Runlett, or his son or Esther Burham, would count the number of boxes and then hand me the money in silver coins. Once in a while, if the Rhode Island Reds were feeling particularly productive, I would come home with a dollar bill.

With this deluge of money pouring in, I went to work making the hen house as attractive as possible for the inmates of my private gold mine. I plugged the holes in the fence and built more nests. A hen can't be lollygagging around in fields and still be doing her job in the coop. I also consulted earnestly with Charley Smart, who sold feed, and he recommended a concoction called "Lay or Bust." I used to wonder about that. Did a poor layer explode right then and there? Bang!

Whatever it comprised, "Lay or Bust" was pretty potent. Egg production picked up amazingly. It became no trick at all to gather up ten dozen eggs for Runlett's store every three or four days. As the piles of silver coins in my top drawer grew each week, I thought seriously of making poultry my life's work. No outgo; all income. The system seemed infallible.

During one three-day period in the spring, my flock crashed through with twenty-four dozen eggs. It was a bonanza. A veritable fortune. As I headed for town in the pony cart, I was trying to multiply twenty-four by fifteen in my head when we reached the mud hole beside Arthur Terri's house. But before I had finished my mathematics, the pony must have sensed romance somewhere ahead; he suddenly broke into a wild gallop, and we went through that mud hole faster than any other vehicle had ever gone. Mud and water flew into the air. The cart lurched wickedly from side to side, and each time it did twenty-four dozen eggs crashed against my feet or the foot rest. Boxes began to fly open, and before we had traveled more than a couple of hundred yards on our mad dash to destiny, twenty-four dozen eggs had emptied their shells into the bottom of the pony cart. This being almost as tight as a boat, the nearly three hundred yolks and whites sloshed, splashed, and slopped around my feet.

All the time, I was hauling at the reins and cursing the pony, chicken farming, and the egg business. Presently the brute began to tire. Romance apparently hadn't been as near as he had thought, for he condescended to stop beside the Chamberlin field.

I paused to consider. Eggs were all right in the pan, but they didn't belong in the bottom of a pony cart or all over my shoes. I scooped up the mess as best I could with the soggy egg boxes and hurled it over a stone wall. After that, I touched up the pony with a good, hard larrup of the reins, and we headed for home.

I gave him another smart larruping before turning him out to pasture, but he probably never did realize that he had put me out of the egg business. Soon after that, we began systematically eating off the flock, and the excess eggs were "put down" in water glass in the vegetable cellar. Thirty-four years later, I hauled them out and took them to the town dump.

However, my mother said that the fifty dollars I'd earned had to go into an account at the Strafford Savings Bank. "If you save one out of every five dollars that you earn throughout your life, you'll end up well-to-do," she said.

Her prediction didn't turn out quite right, but I still have that first fifty dollars. In today's world of free-wheeling finance, it's probably enough to buy a couple dozen eggs.

chapter nineteen

How To Chase Livestock

ALTHOUGH I have been a serious student of Department of Agriculture bulletins for a long time, I have never come across one explaining how to catch a domesticated animal that has escaped from pasture or pen. The department has explored and studied and reported on almost everything else but nary a word on snaring a cow or a pig.

This is a considerable oversight. If cows or pigs are anything like they were fifty years ago, boys all over this great land are still working on the problem alone, without the help they rightfully expect from their government.

Through a quick calculation of the number of persons employed in the department, divided by the number of bulletins published since 1920, I estimate that about five years are spent on each publication before it sees the light of day. This coincides nicely with the five years I devoted to the subject long ago. If the Department of Agriculture cares to take advantage of my experience and prepare a bulletin entitled, perhaps, "Retrieving Your Cow from Mrs. Page's Garden," it knows where to reach me. In the meantime, I'll work up some notes.

As every boy who played nursemaid to a cow in those days knew, a cow operates on a well-understood law of physics: for every action there must be a reaction. Inasmuch as the animal outweighs the boy by seven or eight hundred pounds, he must subdue her by superior mental power.

The best method of dragging one of our docile cows home from Pages' garden was to approach the head and loop a rope around the horns. This established a tentative sort of understanding between the boy and the cow — a hint that something was intended. The idea, if it could be called that, was slow to penetrate through the cow's eyes and ears, down into the jelly that surrounded her brain, and finally to the core of the creature's thinking process. It took time. But once it had been accomplished, and the cow understood that I wished her to move forward, the rest was easy.

She backed up. Dozens of times, I was able to back a cow the entire quarter of a mile home from Mrs. Page's garden by tugging straight ahead on her horns with the rope. She would go through a lot of head-shaking and tacking about, but the course made good was dead astern. That's the sort of bovine psychology that a bulletin writer in the Department of Agriculture needs to know.

The undocile cow, on the other hand, required a different technique. The approach was made from the rear at a high rate of speed. (For short distances I could outrun a cow, particularly if there was an element of surprise in the contest.) There were, and presumably still are, only two handles on a cow feasible for grabbing. One, of course, was the aforementioned horns; the other was the tail. And the latter was the final thing that left Mrs. Page's corn patch. Provided my calculations had been correct, I was attached to it when we came out — having studied the cow mentality, I knew that as long as I pulled back on the tail the animal would move in the opposite direction.

If anybody had put a stopwatch on us between the Pages' and the door of the barn, I think our time would have compared favorably with the world record on a circular track. It was not the most graceful type of locomotion because frequently only my toes were touching the ground, my body leaning against the wind at a forty-five-degree angle. But it was effective.

The third method of instilling a sense of responsibility in a cow was to let her run the long course while I took the short cuts. This was simple geometry. If a cow galloped from A to B to C, I tried to lay my course from A to C. This gave me a readily apparent advantage. By the time the cow was turning the corner in the XYZ dogleg, I would be cutting smartly across from X to Z. If she were impressed enough, she would eventually turn and face me, her sides heaving like bellows. Then I would simply lay a rope around her horns and back her into the barn.

Our cows were not the only ones to break through their fences in order to sample the delights of Mrs. Page's garden. Tater Watson had a couple of fired-up milk factories that often craved to explore the world outside their pasture. When the news reached him, usually by telephone, that his adventurers were roaming through gardens other than his own, he resorted to a straightforward technique. The horns and tails played no role in his cattle roundup; he depended exclusively on his superior athletic prowess to run them down.

He had to get them moving in the right direction, but after that it was man against beast, with no short cuts permitted. Tate just tore after them, shouting and scrambling through the underbrush, until they staggered into their pasture, vanquished. If they lagged on the final stretch, Tate kept them moving by touching their flanks with a stick. To him, cow chasing was a challenge, a contest, and good exercise.

This competitive philosophy got him into trouble one time. He had received the call, and seizing his favorite stick for encouraging his animals, he set off toward Mrs. Page's garden. He and the cow came out of the corn patch at about the same time, Tate pacing himself for the race ahead. They went off on the straightaway for a spell, and then the cow took a turn over a stone wall, crashed through some brush, and headed for our Spring House. The spring itself was covered by some old boards that were showing signs of decay.

Neither the cow nor Tate was aware of this. Even if he had known, Tate's code did not permit him to step off the cow's trail for an instant. When the quarry reached the Spring House, she poked her head through the door for a second and withdrew. Her next maneuver carried her onto the cover of the spring itself, where she made a prodigious leap and landed safely on the other side. Tate, true to his ideals, likewise jumped onto the spring cover and started across. At the center, he sensed that his footing was beginning to descend, so he stopped. That was a fatal decision. If he had kept going, he probably would have made it. But the pause was just long enough for the rotting boards to give way before Tate could scramble back. There were sounds of disintegrating timber, a splash, and a blood-curdling yell; and Tate disappeared from view.

Some idea of the quality of his yell can be gathered from the fact that it carried to our house, a thousand yards off. We all heard it, and presently there were five of us peering down into the spring to see who was bathing in our water supply. The discussion was definitely two sided. I can recall only some of the words. They referred to the condition of the spring cover, the temperature of the water, the cussedness of the cow, and the immediate need for a ladder. Afterward, whenever one of us got thirsty, we'd ask Violet to refill our glass with "a little more Tate, please."

Thus we had four separate ways of persuading a cow to return home in that bygone era. In the past fifty years, new methods may have been developed, but they can be only variations on the basic four.

Pigs were something else again: they had no handles to grab. Moreover, they were smarter than cows. No pig would have let a youngster use that ABC technique more than once. He'd have figured it out. His ploy was to coax his pursuer into following him into what appeared to be a trap, and then turning abruptly and speeding in the opposite direction. You could lunge at him as he dashed by, but, unless you were lucky and caught a leg, he would be gone.

A pig on the loose required teamwork. With four or five people beating the underbrush and shouting advice, commands, and accusations, a pig generally realized that the game was up and trotted back to its pen. This streak of intelligence is what gave us all an athletic Thanksgiving afternoon one year.

John Page's sow had had a litter that spring, and he'd sold two of them to us. The rest he kept for his own use. We put the young pigs in a pen discreetly hidden in a wooded area near the barn. They had a nice shelter and a big patch where they could gambol and root up witch grass and dig. The fence was regulation pig fence, which is to say that the wire ran both horizontally and vertically. Cow wire is single strand, strung from post to post or tree to tree.

The wire around our pigpen was adequate but the installation was faulty. The bottom edge of the wire should have been buried in the ground at least a foot, but nobody ever got around to doing the digging. It was easier and more sporting to round up the pair after they burrowed their way out.

On this particular Thanksgiving afternoon, we were finishing a monstrous meal when something went by outside the window. We established its identity by an almost unanimous shout: "The pigs are out." This was a rallying cry often heard in those days. Specifically, it was a call to action. Only my mother and Aunt Fan failed to join the chase.

The rest of us scrambled out the door, but just during the interval between the alarm and our arrival on the frosty lawn, the escapees had disappeared. We fanned out to reconnoiter the terrain, and in a few minutes Stu located the pigs in the apple orchard. He shouted this intelligence, and we hurried to form ranks and drive them back to their pen.

But they wouldn't drive. No matter how much we yelled and beat the bushes, they kept edging toward the Pages' instead. For once, team play wasn't working. We could get them to head more or less in the direction of the pen, but then they would wheel about and dash through our ranks. This required a regrouping of the hunters, with one of us cutting around the end to hold them at bay until the others could man the flanks.

My father wasn't enjoying the hunt as much as we younger members, and his opinions on pig chasing were expressed freely.

"We may have to shoot them," he said, after slipping on some pine needles and turning his ankle.

But to us, the afternoon's sport was just what was needed after a Thanksgiving dinner. Moreover, the wayward pigs presented a challenge; we'd get them back to their pen if it took all afternoon. It very nearly did. The sun had gone down, and dusk was settling in, when we observed my mother and Aunt Fan walking up the driveway. There was something odd about their expressions, and they could barely keep from laughing. We paused in our chase long enough to see what was so funny.

"Why don't you try driving them the other way?" my mother said.

My father was in no mood for teasing. He rubbed his sore ankle and said, "Because we can't leave them out all night. They'd freeze to death."

"We don't need four pigs," my mother said.

All of us exclaimed, "*Four* pigs?"

"These two, and the two back in the pen," she said.

"What do you mean, the two in the pen?" my father demanded.

"Go see for yourself," Aunt Fan put in. "I know a pig when I see one. I know *two* pigs when I see them."

"You've been chasing John Page's pigs all afternoon," my mother said, and then the two ladies could control their mirth no longer.

It took us a while to join in the fun, but, after we returned home and examined the pigpen, the afternoon's recreation did appear to have its light side. Four closely related pigs did look pretty much alike. We had naturally assumed that the pigs going by the dining-room window were ours; it just didn't occur to us that the Pages' porkers also went off on an occasional stroll.

Which leads us to the final rule about pig chasing as it was practiced many years ago.

Don't chase the wrong ones.

chapter twenty

My Enemy, the Cow

No cow I had anything to do with ever died while under my care. They did not even get sick. Cows belonging to neighbors expired right and left from eating bicycle pumps and rubber inner tubes. John Page's cow caught her horns in a barbed-wire fence and promptly toppled over and broke her neck. On the Morses' place, a mile away, a cow attempted to explore the bottom of a well and wasn't discovered until the following spring.

Our cows had been part of the war effort. The intention, as explained to me, was that this merry band would produce milk, butter, and cheese in sizable quantities by eating hay and grass.

Then these dairy products would be consumed by the civilian population of New Hampshire, who in turn would gain enough strength to carry on at home, as they say. Eventually, through a long and complicated process, this would bring about the downfall of the Kaiser and restore democracy to the world.

Anyway, that's the way my father explained it to me when I was seven. Throughout the war, our Shankhassick dairy retailed milk in the village of Durham for exactly half the price of its production. Reliable Will Burroughs, the hired man, took care of the dairy, and the Hun was on the run.

When the war ended, most of the herd was sold. Will departed, and the tradition of the family cow reared its ugly head. As a result, four remained: Spicy Peach, Mundell, Horizon, and Venus. They were Ayrshires — and with all due respect to their breed association, this type was pretty odd, to say the least. Just an average one could outrun a horse, jump higher than a gazelle, and toss a dairyman more than twenty feet with her horns. They were marked with brown and white patches, and their forward armor made the Texas Longhorn look like a runt.

From 1920 through 1924, these four misfits and I joined our lives in one long vendetta. My brothers had intelligently discovered that their interests lay elsewhere. My father had lost interest and had returned to writing books, which was judicious in view of the cow damages that frequently had to be paid to Mrs. Page for her garden.

At the age of ten anything looks possible. I thought I could tame Spicy Peach. In the parlance of the trade, she was known as a fence-jumper. Old Mundell floundered over fences like a full-rigged ship striking a bar, and Horizon depended on speed and momentum to carry her over, but Spicy had her own tactics. She did not admit that the fence was there. She walked stolidly ahead until something gave way. Venus compromised by remaining outside the fence most of the time.

In Spicy's case, a friendly neighbor thought he could solve the problem of her fence jumping. "Drag her," he said. So I dragged her, according to his instructions. I located twenty-five feet of chain and made it fast to a ten-foot log. Then, just before Spicy went barreling out of the barn and into the pasture, I tied a stout rope around her horns.

Although Spicy had taken a considerable interest in the log and the chain, she apparently did not connect them with the rope around her horns. Once clear of the barn door, she let out a cheerful bleat and headed for the lower pasture. She covered the first twenty-five feet rapidly enough, then fetched up short as the chain snapped taut. The resulting shock would have broken the neck of any breed less hardy and robust than an Ayrshire.

But Spicy merely picked herself up from the ground, directed a new and respectful look toward the log, and set out again for the lower pasture. This time, there were only five or six feet of slack to take up, but these were enough to bring her to her knees, bellowing. Now, though, she had established a relationship between the log and herself, so she adopted a new tack. Putting her great head down, she moved gingerly to the end of the chain and began to pull. After all, the oxen that helped build New Hampshire had been only slightly larger than she. In a moment she had mastered the engineering principles involved and was plodding resolutely after the other cows. That evening, when she returned to the barn to be milked, she had added two hundred feet of wire fence to her drag.

It was not long before she was dragging around a couple of democrat-wagon wheels, an old grindstone, and parts of a windmill fan. She made a pretty sight coming up the pasture with these pieces of farm hardware skipping along behind her. Believers as well as skeptics turned up from miles around to watch.

Then, in the spring of 1922, she got the taxes raised. According to an old New Hampshire custom the town selectmen go a-viewing early in March. They view your property, find out how you voted in the previous election, and evaluate your holdings on the basis of your doughnuts and coffee.

In this particular year they viewed the house and the coffeepot, then set out to view the barn. They chose to do this from the southeast corner at about the same time that Spicy came around the northeast end, towing her junk yard. At the sight of so much authority Spicy came to a full stop, then cut to her right. The selectmen cut to their left. The barnyard was six inches deep in spring mud.

Afterward, my father apologized, swore that he had voted the Republican ticket since the age of ten, and hurled a fairly hefty rock in the direction of the retreating Spicy. But it was no good. The taxes went up the following year.

It was my belief then, and it still is, that each cow has some endearing quality that makes her remembered long after she has passed away. Mundell, the eldest, for example, was a foot-stepper. Once she had placed her size-twelve hoof on the human instep she went into a trance. She lost touch with ordinary events. If she could have managed it, she probably would have tried to get all of her weight onto that one hoof. But she couldn't. Therefore, she made the best of what she had. She froze.

I could kick with my other foot. I could pummel with my fist until it turned blue. Shouts, cries, and threats fell on deaf ears. Eventually she might forget what she was doing and shift her weight, but if she did it was simply an oversight.

Horizon, on the other hand, made spectacular use of her horns. Generally, it was just good, clean Ayrshire fun. Except on those rare occasions when she got to thinking about something else, she caught me directly above the seventh rib morning and night for four years.

Venus was never much of a problem, because she preferred the open range of Durham Point. During her so-called dry periods she went native in this area, and only a prolonged safari on ponyback ever brought her back in the fall. In 1923 I failed to find any trace of her. About Christmas time my father casually asked what had become of Venus. I said I didn't know. Then he shook his head dubiously and declared, "I always did think she was half caribou."

That closed the discussion for thirty years. At the end of this unperturbed wait, Tater Watson finally disclosed Venus's fate. "Elmer shot and et her," he confided cheerfully. Elmer lived two farms farther down the road. The record remained intact: no cow of mine ever died of natural causes.

Thus by 1924 my herd was down to three cows. Although Mundell was growing weary of the struggle, the other two continued to skirmish. Horizon, just now hitting her prime, had gone dry for good. Spicy had become inoperative in one spigot after a good-natured brush with barbed wire. Despite this, however, there was still plenty of milk for everybody.

Morning and night, the cream separator whined in the kitchen and the skim was sloshed down the drain. But even in those uninflationary days our milk was probably costing thirty cents a quart.

During those five memorable years the routine was constant. When the cows were let out to pasture each day in the summer, the same Ayrshire ritual took place: every morning Spicy and Horizon attempted to squeeze through the barn door at the same instant. Spicy invariably came out of her stall under full steam, slipped, and went down on her side. She always suspected foul play, for she would glare balefully at me, dig her great horns into the nearest object, and then scramble to her feet. Having dropped behind because of this maneuver, she then tried to make up for lost time. She bolted for the door with her head down, only to discover that Horizon was blocking the way. To give Spicy credit, she did attempt to stop, but her momentum carried them both into the barnyard like coal running down a chute.

While all this was going on, other and older agriculturists were having better luck than I. Farther down the road a cow stepped into a quicksand pit. Still others ate too many bolts and old shoes and expired with dignity in their stalls. Elmer, the neighbor who "et" Venus, lost one in the river.

It was a time of change. Some advanced thinkers even probed the idea of selling off their family herds. When these progressives were not immediately struck by lightning, others began to take an interest. A neighboring city had spawned a dairy plant, and the milk was said to test higher than the homegrown variety. In the case of Shankhassick milk, this was believable. More than once our milk came to the table after Spicy had planted her right hind foot in the full pail.

My own feelings about cow care deteriorated even further when I approached the age of fourteen. One day when I went to school, the prettiest girl in the room exclaimed, "Phew, who brought the cow to class?"

That did it. From then on pressure was stepped up to get rid of the beasts. I went to some lengths at dinnertime to point out that (1) this was 1924, (2) the family herd was passing out of the picture, and (3) I would personally walk to town each day and buy the milk.

My father played coy for a long time. It was hard for him to break with tradition. At one moment he would raise my hopes by saying, "I guess I'll have to go up to Epping to see Mr. Yeaton." Mr. Yeaton bought and sold cattle. Then, a couple of days later, he would gaze fondly at the full milk pitcher and guess that perhaps he would let only Horizon go because she was so obviously unproductive.

My spirits rose and fell with these observations. About a week before my fourteenth birthday, the world went black. At dinner my father announced that he had looked at the problem from all angles and had decided to keep the whole herd after all.

What would we do if there were a famine, he wanted to know? With milk from Spicy and Mundell, and by eating Horizon, we could live on for quite a long time. Somehow, I must have missed the twinkle in his eye when he made these remarks.

A week later, on my fourteenth birthday, there were no presents. I ransacked the house, but the astonishing truth was there. They had forgotten the date.

With nothing better to do, I plodded out to tackle the chores. When I got to the barn there was an ominous silence about it — no clanging horns, or scrabbling hoofs, or moaning animals trying to digest old doorknobs. A closer look revealed that the stanchions were shut the way I had left them the previous evening, only then they had had cows in them.

Now, in her heyday Spicy had been able to open her stanchion by banging around with her horns until she hit the catch, but even she had never been able to close it up again. That plodding Mundell or skittish Horizon had been able to accomplish the trick was unthinkable. I ran out of the barn to look at the pasture.

It was then that I saw a note tacked to the door. "Happy birthday, son," it read. "We gave the cows away."

There have been many birthday presents since then, but none to equal that wonderful, that incredible, that joyous and eternal silence that Spicy, old Mundell, and the useless Horizon left behind them that morning in 1924.

chapter twenty-one
Life in the Village

FOR three months one winter, we moved into the center of the village. As a group, we weren't easy to move. In addition to the usual household impediments, we traveled with three cows, a pony, some stray poultry, and Bridget the pregnant Irish terrier. Neither the livestock nor we had ever had it so good.

The stables were paneled with varnished fir. The box stall for the pony was finished similarly, with a private chute from the hayloft. The adjoining carriage room was resplendent in shiny paneling, and the hayloft was a dog's delight for Bridget and her forthcoming issue. About fifty feet behind the barn, the hens had the run of a luxurious house that measured forty feet in length and twenty in width.

Inside the big colonial house, the comforts were no less astonishing. A few years before, Charles Hoitt, the former owner, had been seized with an insatiable desire to keep up with the Smiths.

Hamilton Smith had returned to town after an obviously successful career in mining, particularly diamond mining. He promptly began doing what every boy dreamed about in those days: he built the finest establishment in town. It contained a bona fide ballroom — not just an area where the rugs were rolled up when the dancing began. No, this room was constructed solely for pretty women and gallant men, and for the waltz. Mr. Smith named his enormous home Red Tower because the ballroom rose so high in the air. Surrounding all this magnificence were a separate billiard house, a caretaker's home, a stable, and living quarters for a coachman. Behind these, the manicured land sloped gently down to the mill pond and about a mile along the Oyster River. Here several men were employed on an annual basis to cut the brush and trim the trees. In time, it became known as Smith Park, and it was open to everybody.

For those who wanted to contemplate nature from a sitting position, Hamilton Smith built small summer houses on the rocks that bordered the water. The town did not have an Episcopal church then, so he had his own built in the park. It had stained-glass windows and beautifully hand-worked pews. Down on the saltwater river, he constructed a boathouse. This was unheard of. In it he kept a naphtha launch and a catboat named the *Joy*. (The latter was his eventual undoing. With some friends one afternoon, he ran aground about two miles downriver, and while attempting to get the *Joy* free he died of a heart attack. A polished granite marker still marks the spot where this occurred.)

Now, the remarkable thing about Hamilton Smith's short but lively stay in the village was that almost nobody resented his good fortune. He came back to town, made a magnificent splash, and shared his ballroom, his billiard house, his chapel, his park, and his boats with anybody who cared to use them.

Seemingly the only person who was embittered by this sudden and startling opulence was Charles Hoitt. He knew that he couldn't match it, but he would give it a try. So he called in some carpenters to remodel his fine colonial home. They removed the hand-planed paneling over the fireplaces and replaced it with white oak. They constructed a white-oak stairway to the second floor, and threw out the old-fashioned one that had served so well since 1790. All of the delicate moldings and graceful wainscoting on the first floor were yanked out and brought up to date with white oak.

Charles Hoitt had likewise been introduced to the tile fireplaces at Red Tower. As a consequence, the aging red bricks of his four fireplaces were covered over with greenish tile. Then, for good measure, he added something that put him a little ahead. In the spacious front hallway, he ripped out the plaster and replaced it with sheet tin on which designs of flowers had been pressed. It was new, it was atrocious, and Hamilton Smith didn't have it.

The sparkling quarters in which the cows and the pony now found themselves also resulted from the influence of Mr. Smith. The interior of his stable was finished in varnished fir paneling. Mr. Hoitt rebuilt *his* barn to the same specifications.

There wasn't much he could do about competing with Hamilton Smith in the way of furniture. As a mining engineer, the latter had collected his from all parts of the world. All Charles Hoitt had were some old family pieces dating to 1750. Highboys, lowboys, four-posters, mahogany secretaries, and the like. But Mr. Hoitt knew that a new era was approaching, and that it was time to make a change. All the antiques went to the attic for storage, and the period of overstuffed furniture arrived in town.

It is inconceivable that a more homely or more comfortable truckload of furniture was ever assembled under one roof, at least in Durham. To us boys who had spent all our young lives sitting on ladderbacks and Early American chairs with wooden seats, this was an impressive improvement. One of the couches, which was covered with orange material, became known as "the wallow." Its magnificent springs didn't start to stiffen until the human body had sunk into them six inches.

The house was therefore comfortable to live in, provided you didn't think what it must have been like before Charles Hoitt took it into the twentieth century.

For a while, this cosmopolitan living where there were street lights and sidewalks was great stuff. The movie house was just around the corner, and at that time it was running some pretty exciting films. Many of its features concerned brave, intrepid sled dogs of the north. Nor were there many subtitles to bother with. An occasional "mush" was about all that was necessary to keep the plot going. Sometimes, Stu and

147

I would sit through the second show and outline the story to anybody who cared to listen.

But it was the gymnasium at the college that caught our attention the most. It was located only a short distance up Main Street, and here during the winter months a fascinating game called basketball was played every other Saturday night. What a sport it was! Excitement, a lot of rushing around, cheering, and crowds going wild.

Every town kid who could escape from home made his way to the gymnasium at seven o'clock. We would sit glassy-eyed through the first half, then get to work on the real reason behind our enthusiasm for basketball. This was called scrambling for pennies, and it was part of the evening's entertainment. Twenty or thirty of us would march onto the floor and fight and wrestle and snatch for the pennies that the college audience flipped down from the balcony.

Every member of the undergraduate body carried a jackknife in his back pocket then. In another pocket he carried a few matches. By opening the blade of the knife, he was able to devise a perfect platform for holding a penny while he heated it with a match. This is what made scrambling so interesting: we never knew whether we were going to pick up a cold penny or a hot one. In the event that it was the latter, Chickie Hatch or Squeaky Perley or somebody would yell, "Hot one!" and cup his hand over it long enough for it to cool. According to the unofficial rules of the game, the penny was his, and the others went off scrambling somewhere else.

Somehow, my brothers and I had neglected to tell our parents the real nature of our new-found devotion to the sport of basketball. We suspected that they would object to our pastime. Eventually, this suspicion was proved correct.

Mon Whitney set the stage. He and I were wrestling over a penny one night, when I got the first clue that it had recently been held in a jackknife. I hollered the customary "Hot one!" and cupped my hand over it. Anybody else would have honored the rules and gone off to scramble for another one, but Mon's instincts weren't always the highest. Instead of conceding the contest, he brought his right foot down on my hand and pressed it against the sizzling penny. Whoever heated that one must have used several matches, because it produced a spat of pain in the middle of my palm. I hit Mon as hard as I could with my left hand, and he removed his foot and went off to scramble on the other end of the gymnasium.

Right then and there, my fondness for basketball diminished. By the time I got home I had a perfect facsimile of Abraham Lincoln blistering on my palm. It's hard to hide something as interesting as that. My mother noted it the next morning at breakfast. Under different circumstances I would have attempted a lie, but when a likeness of Abe Lincoln shows up on your skin, it's pretty hard to argue that you burned your hand on the stove.

So I told her the truth, and she called Doctor Grant and also my father, and between the three of them they dissuaded me from any further competition at the college gymnasium. If anybody should ask me today how many men there are on a basketball team, I couldn't tell him, but I am an authority on penny scrambling.

Perhaps that episode was the beginning of my disenchantment with town life. In any case, early in March certain signs of homesickness began to appear in our over-stuffed household. Almost every day, somebody felt it necessary to travel the two miles to the farm to check on things. That was just a camouflage for wanting to get back to the river and the stone walls and the woods. The bright lights were beginning to pall. Besides, spring was in the air. Bridget and her newborn puppies were yearning for horizons less restricted than Charles Hoitt's hayloft. The cows needed exercise after three months in their varnished boudoir, and Main Street was not much of a pasture, even in those days. My brother and I were also beginning to feel confined. There wasn't a good woodchuck hole within a mile, and how could we tell whether it was really spring unless we were able to spot a freshly opened den? Until we found one of these, winter was still officially with us.

So during the last two weeks of March, we moved our personal belongings back home. Everybody remarked on the amount of stuff that one family had managed to collect in three short months. Magazines, books, Christmas presents, and numerous editions of the *New York Times*. We weren't a family that parted with things casually.

The livestock had also increased in numbers. Counting the ten puppies and two calves born during the winter, plus the flock in the palatial chicken house, we made quite an impression on the final day of March as the pony towed the cows and their offspring down Main Street, past the church, and onto the Durham Point Road. If we had not been so recognizable, townspeople might have suspected that a bunch of gypsies was passing through. The Irish terrier and her brood gamboled alongside the pony cart, ecstatic in their new world. The crated fowl cackled and squawked and shed their feathers. Bringing up the rear were my father and mother in the car, watching for strays. The top was down, and on the back seat was the orange-colored "wallow." This was the only concession they would make to Charles Hoitt's era of luxury.

That night we sat cheerfully on our ladderbacks and our hardseated Early American chairs. It was so good to be home again. Once again we could look out in the dark and not see a light, or hear an automobile or the sound of feet on the sidewalk.

For Stu and me, the winter in town had been a broadening experience. We had seen how the city folk lived. When something had been needed in the kitchen, we had simply walked across the street to Sam Runlett's store and got it. We had become familiar with every celluloid sled dog of the north. We knew about pennies on a gymnasium floor.

But none of these attainments could hold a candle to riding ice cakes down the river, or opening up our secret trails in the pine woods.

Fifty years later, I still feel that way.

About the Author

In 1907, a writer named Ralph D. Paine bought a tidewater farm in Durham, New Hampshire. He called it Shankhassick, or "wild goose," the Indian name for the river that bordered it. The farm was a place to settle down, to write, and to rear a daughter and four sons.

The youngest boys, Philbrook and Stuart, were born in 1910. They grew up at Shankhassick, and when Phil Paine later followed his father into writing, one of his favorite subjects was the farm where he spent his boyhood and where eventually he returned to live. Shankhassick provided grist for weekly columns in the *New Hampshire Sunday News*; articles in *Yankee,* the *Atlantic Monthly,* and *New Hampshire Profiles*; and two books, *Report From the Village* and *Squarely Behind the Beavers.* Finally, toward the end of his life, Phil sat down to write the story of that enchanted, exciting era when Shankhassick joined the twentieth century. The result is *The Best of Times.*

Phil attended Phillips Andover Academy and the University of New Hampshire. During World War II he skippered a supply-and-rescue boat in the South Pacific. A tall, kind, wonderfully strong, intensely private man, he was a freethinker and a gentleman. Above all things, he loved working in the woods and messing about with boats, and one of his proudest possessions was the great oak dock he built on the river. Like Grandfather's clock, it succumbed to the elements about the same time he did, in June of 1978.

Phil's wife Serena, his daughter, his son-in-law, and his granddaughter still live at Shankhassick.